THE HOPE AT THE END OF THE TUNNEL

A memoir about love, sorrow
and rediscovering joy

Erica Hansen

For Jer - I wrote our story, babe, just like you wanted.
For Victoria - My astonishing ray of sunshine.

Introduction

On March 2, 2020 I made the following post on Facebook.

There's a great quote: "I don't know what I think until I read what I say."

Yesterday marked two years since my amazing Jeramy died suddenly hurling me down a new life path. As soon as I saw that daunting road stretched out in front of me, I said "I need paper and a pen."

I sat there in that moment knowing the only way I could try to make sense of the pain was to write. And I've been doing so ever since.

I write at the cemetery. I write sipping coffee. I write on vacations. In the early stages, I wouldn't even leave the house without my journal as I was afraid I'd be paralyzed without it.

Slowly, that anxiety lifted and it became my refuge and respite every night. I couldn't sleep without hearing the pen drag across the pages.

Then I worried it'd be journal after journal of reading 'I'm so sad.' I challenged my brain to be more creative with its expressions – dabbling in poetry and song lyrics which then led to teaching myself how to play guitar (still very much a beginner).

These pages contain tears, wine drips, coffee stains, even chocolate frosting. They contain sketches of headstones, diagrams of new grief illustrations, anger, confusion and loneliness.

They also contain countless moments of love, laughter, support and amazing gestures of kindness that have also moved me to tears.

Jeramy was the most extraordinary individual in every way. I love him deeply and learned from him daily.

But for those of you wondering how I'm doing, that's how I'm doing - so I thought I'd write about it. And I love you for asking.

All of those journals - those thoughts and musings turned into this book. I've spent the time since Jer's passing trying to put words to how I'm feeling; to flex my creative muscles so as not to lose that side of my brain; to capture the odd and bizarre moments that happen to a person navigating the landmine of grief, pain and loss.

Jeramy always wanted us to 'write our story' so I have. Though it didn't have the ending we both envisioned.

I hope I can promise it's not all sad. What I *can* promise is getting to know Jeramy will be worth your time.

DRESSES

I have these two great black dresses and I'm not sure what to do with them. One is a fab faux-wrap dress, slim-fit, boat neck, ¾ sleeve in a jersey fabric. The other is a wrap shirt-dress, gorgeous full skirt, tie at the waist, almost looks like it was tailored for me.

I love them both and felt great in them both. Now they hang in the back corner of the closet, a visible layer of dust gathering on the shoulder. I don't wear them and I don't get rid of them.

I wore the first dress to my husband's viewing. I wore the second to his funeral, to stand in front of the hundreds gathered to tell them what an extraordinary husband he was.

How do you get rid of a dress like that? A dress that stood up with you, wrapped around you when you needed it. A dress that helped you feel presentable when you were anything but. A dress that you happened to buy a while back never knowing you'd be reaching for it at a time you needed something decent to wear yet could never have gone shopping to find it.

They feel significant and yet I tell myself it's just fabric.

Don't let the funeral scare you. I used to stand reading the backs of books and anytime they dealt with death or dying I'd roll my eyes and put them down, and look for something... different? Lighter? Not as scary maybe? I'll admit, in the search for all the whys, I've even wondered if that's a why - my avoidance of the topic meant I had to learn more about it - in the most difficult way possible.

This story isn't about a death. I mean, it is. But I want to introduce you to my sweetheart and I can't do it by having you fall in love with him then killing him off at the end. That's cruel (trust me, I know).

This story is about navigating life after a loss. More importantly, it's about rebirth, it's about falling apart and looking around you to find the people in your world holding the pieces to put you back together again. It's about a poignant, painful sadness that tickles the back of your brain during the happiest and strangest of moments. It's about all-consuming peace that surfaces when you pause to give thanks for the gift of time. It's about discovering. It's about coping.

And it's about the most beautiful love story, mostly, never told.

MEET CUTE

We sat on Kirsten's front porch, the setting sun lit up the empty wine bottles; the party lights flickered on as the long July day drew to a close.

"They have the best 'meet cute' story - the best," she said to Mel, her friend who had joined us.

"We do, it's true," I smiled.

"How? How'd you meet you have to tell me," Mel poured herself another and settled in to hear the story.

"We met at Costco."

"WHAT?! Costco?! Were you both working there or something?"

Kirsten laughed, "No she didn't work there."

"But how else do you meet someone at Costco?" Mel responded, looking back and forth between the two of us.

"Right? I know," I said and joined her in another glass. "I went to Costco on a Sunday, late morning like I always did. I don't even think I had showered yet for the day," they nodded in understanding.

My mind flashed back to that time in my life, feeling alone and isolated at the end of a marriage, divorce on the horizon, handling the household tasks by myself with a preschooler, the perpetual scowl I likely carried on my face daily.

"I was pushing Victoria, my daughter, through the store and it's not like I was out there trying to meet someone, if you know what I mean. I was not in the best place emotionally."

"Totally," Kirsten chimed in.

"So we passed Jeramy in the last freezer aisle, he had his two girls in the cart, and he just beamed at me. Beamed! And I thought 'what the hell is this guy's problem?!?"

They both laughed and said "right!??!" in unison.

"We sort of zig-zagged past each other all the way down all those Costco aisles," I said, drawing zig-zags in the air for emphasis.

"It was so dumb," I went on. "I tried to act interested in buckets of soy sauce and crap. I tried to avoid him but each aisle there he was."

"Did he ever say anything?" Mel asked.

"Oh he made a few jokes from time to time. It was funny cause each time he did, his oldest daughter, I think she was 10, would roll her eyes at him. She'd be like…" I demonstrated the embarrassed-by-her-dad eye roll.

"So we got all the way down into the supplement section and he finally said 'I'm Jeramy, by the way' and I said 'I'm Erica, it's nice to meet you' and that was it."

"That was it?"

"Yep, we went our separate ways and I didn't think much of it. Well the next day, that Monday at work, I got a friend request from him on Facebook."

"Wait what?!" Mel almost shouted and gestured big enough her wine nearly slipped out of the top of her glass. "How?! Did you tell him your last name?"

"Nope - he must've just typed in Erica and - well you know

Facebook, it's quick to try to figure out who's named Erica in your area. We did end up having a few mutual friends as well but he just looked me up and I must've pulled right up."

Both women sat smiling and sipping, "wow" one of them said.

"I rolled my eyes. I mean 'Seriously?! You can't just chat with someone in a grocery store, now you have to be FRIENDS with them?!'"

"Right?!" they chimed in.

"It seemed so dumb and I don't friend people I don't know anyway. So I ignored the request for about a week.

"Annnnyway, I don't know why, but I nosed through his profile and he looked normal, most importantly. He seemed fun and his girls were cute so I accepted the friend request and that was it."

"Did he start messaging you like crazy?" Mel asked.

"Actually no. Not at all. We swapped a few 'hi how are yous?', but that was it. I was in the midst of figuring out the whole divorce process and just not interested."

"Really?"

"I mean, it's interesting cause he would later say he just had a feeling it wasn't time yet."

"Wow"

"So that went on for a year and half," I explained.

"Wait, you met him a year and a half before anything happened?!"

"I know - it's bizarre. I mean, we'd like pictures from time to time, I think there was a birthday message in there but that was it. So during that time I was divorcing and regrouping and all of that and one day he posts of pic of himself in costume and tagged Utah Opera in the photo."

"The opera?!"

"I know! I thought 'that Costco guy sings??' cause I sing so that caught my interest. And I just thought 'huh... that does not fit the profile I'd created in my mind for him. I mean snow mobiler, party on a boat type of guy - yes but not an opera kind of guy."

"You said he was in costume, right? Did he sing?"

"Well not entirely but that's when I sent him a message on Facebook and said 'do you sing? Do you perform?' And he likes to say 'you cracked the door open and I burst through like the Kool-Aid man!'" Both Kirsten and Mel laughed and nodded enthusiastically.

"Well he didn't sing, but when the opera does a large-scale production and they need big crowd scenes they hire extras, put them in costume to play the townsfolk. So he was cast as a sailor in Madame Butterfly."

"Oh wow, that's cool!"

"Isn't that neat?" Kirsten said toward Mel.

"Jer said he always wanted to know what it felt like to perform," I added. "He wanted to do the musicals in high school but he did sports and there wasn't time to do both, but he always wanted that experience. Well he absolutely loved everything about performing. He was the first one on stage and he walked out as a sailor checking out the village and stuff. It's funny too because my friend and her mom went to that opera and they absolutely remembered that cutie sailor who walked out on stage first."

"That's amazing."

"Anyway, he asked if I saw the production but I'd been out of town for the whole run so I didn't. But I did say that we need to meet for a churro soon - cause you know Costco and all - and I wanted to hear about his experience."

"And that was it?," Mel asked.

"That was it. We messaged a few more times then one day he's like 'I'm going to Costco today and I can bring you a churro.'"

"To work?" Mel was surprised.

"Crazy, right?" Kirsten agreed.

"Yes and you know I work at the Zoo and it's not near anything and it's not on the way to anything it's just way out there. So I thought I'd call his bluff and I said okay."

"Did he bring them?" Mel asked.

"He did!" Kirsten chimed in

"He did - He brought two - one for me and one for Victoria. And the rest is pretty much history, as they say," I added. "We went on our first date shortly after then we were pretty much together."

We wrapped up the remaining food, collected the empty bottles.

"I told you it was the best meet cute story - so cute," Kirsten said.

Mel agreed, "so cute."

I gathered my glass and and the last few dishes and listened to their conversation as they walked inside, "don't you think that should be in a movie?"

DICHOTOMY OF JER

Jeramy was a larger-than-life walking dichotomy: two things that one would think were mutually exclusive; that could not nor should not exist at the same time, in the same person, that was Jer.

And it's important you know that to get the full scope of all that he was. If I told you he was a motorcycle guy that would conjure up one mental image. If I told you he was an opera-lover that would conjure up someone completely different.

Your image for the man who makes chocolate chip cookies for his daughters, would be different from what your mind would dream up for a man who wore that Borat wrestling/underwear thing to make his friends laugh on a trip to Lake Powell.

He was a rugby/football playin' man's-man, but loved doing laundry and wanted his clothes to smell better than anyone else's. He also promised me I'd never have to do laundry again (yes, I'm still bitter about that one.)

He was a risky snowmobiler but bought 'Live, Laugh, Love' candles and other various home decor.

He'd meet his buddies for drinks and cigars but would get all of us up and out of the house for church.

He was a naturally gifted athlete, but also loved musicals.

He was born and raised in Salt Lake City, Utah yet also fluent in Spanish.

He was beautifully passionate but equally relished singing duets with me.

He was a force of confidence - whether protecting his family or surpassing his sales goals, but there were times he also needed me to run my fingers through his hair and tickle his face.

He loved NASCAR and driving fast cars but just as eagerly drove Golden Girl (my minivan), washed her, kept her clean and kept her oil changed. He would swap me cars for the day, do all the car maintenance on Goldie then bring her home all detailed with a full tank of gas.

He was a superstar at work but signed up to be a Tupperware rep because he was sure he could sell that stuff and bring in a decent side income (he was going to be the Tupperware Hunk).

He enjoyed irreverent humor with his buddies but also readily gave them sound advice when life tossed them around.

He was whiskey and ice cream.

He was Van Halen and Celine Dion.

He was watching Breaking Bad and The Bachelor.

He could throw down the Haka and could nail every line of Daddy Warbucks' in Annie.

Jeramy was the most charming bundle of incongruities. The best part? He was completely unapologetic. He didn't care if his buddies razzed him, he wasn't embarrassed to drive a minivan, he proudly told people they ought to check out opera. He even gave tips on doing laundry. It was just Jer and everyone loved him for it - the athletes, the singers, the motorcycle dudes, the moms, the car guys - they were drawn to his exuberance, joy and willingness to participate. Jer had a little something he could share with everyone, and he did so, freely.

HERMOSA DONETTE

Falling in love with Jeramy Evans was the single easiest thing I have ever done. It happened before I knew it; it happened while I was avoiding it; it happened because it couldn't *not* happen. To know him was to love him, cliché as it sounds.

As I write this, it's been three years. Jer has now officially been gone as long as I knew him. We dated roughly 1 ½ years and were married 1 ½ years. The fiery fury with which he lived his life and packed his minutes leaves me feeling like the road runner, or coyote or whichever one was left standing in the middle of the road in a swirl of smoke, blinking and wondering what just happened. That was my time with Jer - fast, energetic and gone in the blink of an eye as I just sit here looking around, wondering what happened.

"I'm in the south side of the Costco parking lot in a white Nissan Altima"

Oh sheesh, I'm going to have to tell him I drive a minivan!???!!? Hmmm…. We were headed downtown but arranged to meet at Costco, naturally, to condense cars. I'd heard that's how first dates happen these days (can't have him knowing where you live) and I was living with my parents at the time, still getting back on my feet after my divorce.

"Okay, but I have to warn you I'm driving a gold minivan"

"Excellent, I have the seat warmer on for you!" *He has the seat warmer on for me? Okay this guy's good.*

I loved seat warmers. Beyond that, he didn't seem to care one iota that I was in a minivan.

He was outside of his car waiting for me, gave me a big classic Jeramy hug and opened the car door for me, apologizing that his car was dirty (it wasn't).

At first, the evening felt like a movie almost - like watching the events in third person. I didn't recognize myself here in this unfamiliar car with this boyish, energetic man. I was simply out of practice.

I asked about his daughters before we even got on the freeway. He lit up with joy talking about their personalities and activities. His four year old is a spitfire and his older daughter had just started 5th grade. Jeramy, wearing a hip white button-down, jeans and a leather jacket, chuckled heartily, while telling me about the discomfort of the 5th graders during her maturation program earlier that day.

He loves his daughters = check

I told him about my sweet Victoria, the little gal he saw sitting in my shopping cart at Costco. She was seven and had a heart full of song and an incredible imagination. We both noted what nice ages our daughters were - 4, 7 and 11.

We had a good laugh about our text exchange a week prior, when he asked me out. We had been texting a little bit here and there after his churro delivery. One night, I was shopping at Costco and texted him "I guess you're not here shopping tonight?" - trying to be playful. He immediately texted back that he was not at Costco but joked that his plan had worked beautifully because

I'm thinking about him. His next text said, "Would you like to Hermosa Donette with me on Wednesday"

"Would I like to what??" I typed back, resting my elbows on the shopping cart near the tables with the folded piles of clothes.

"Haha what the???.. Would you like to get dinner with me on Wednesday?" he responded.

He changed lanes for our upcoming freeway exit and laughed, explaining he used voice text and his phone was set to do both English and Spanish. Turns out he spent two years in Argentina on a service mission for his church. He was fluent in Spanish and apparently his phone was too. Siri took his voice text and auto-corrected to "Hermosa Donette." He quickly mentioned that hermosa donette means 'my beautiful, my love,' giving me a quick glance.

After a quick bite of pizza, we were off to see Trans-Siberian Orchestra in concert. Now, fast forward a little bit and we chuckled at that first-date choice. Jer was a rocker through and through. While I love great musicianship, this is a concert best enjoyed with the protection of earplugs, in my opinion. TSO was out on their regular seasonal tour, and their stop in Utah was in early November. We had great seats and Jer sat there full of excitement, anticipation and gusto.

Being from Salt Lake City, there is one fundamental thing you need to know before forging ahead with dating which is - are you Mormon / LDS. Mormons are wonderful. But it would be difficult to go beyond a first date if one person is Mormon and one is not - it's a fundamental religious/lifestyle difference that could make life more difficult.

My litmus test to casually get to the bottom of this: Offer to buy him a beer. So, before the concert started, I went to the bathroom. I texted him: "Do you drink? Can I buy you a beer? Ice cream? Now's your last chance!" If he chose the ice cream, he's Mormon. If he chose the beer, he's not.

His response: "Ha! Okay, I'll have a Bud Light" *YES!* "Do you want me to come carry them?" *Bonus point.* "No I think I've got it."

Once we were dating he told me how delighted he was that I thought to do that - thought about him, offered to buy, delivered with a smile. It's still the best beer I ever bought.

We drank our beers and the show got going. Jer loved it! Electric guitars, pyrotechnics, some Christmas dragon thing that we'd chuckle about for months to come. He put his arm around me, I nestled closer. It was…. nice. Loud, but nice.

I was on a date and it was fun. He was fun. I guess divorced people with kids can still have fun - who knew?

He dropped me off at the Costco parking lot, gave me another big hug, got me safely in my minivan and sent me on my way.

He texted right away and said he wanted to do it again soon and he even mentioned he liked my minivan. I responded, "Well it doesn't give me the elegant sophisticated image I try to project, but we like her too."

As the beginning stage unfolded, fresh into my own new life as a single, divorced woman, I was determined to control the pace of this. I was determined not to 'end up with a boyfriend.' I envisioned myself on lots of dates with lots of men and nary a care. Just…. you know… a true single gal who no one could pin down.

Jeramy asked me out again right away. He didn't worry about looking too eager; he didn't follow some unwritten rule of waiting a certain amount of time before texting - he just wanted me to know he liked me and wanted to spend more time with me.

I tried to dilly-dally a bit. I acted busy on a few nights - too available. I didn't ask him to my company work party - too soon. I kept him to a few lunch dates instead of dinner dates - less romantic. But each time I'd get in my car afterward and think *'damn! I like him.'*

Jer invited me over for tea, one evening. *'Oh is that what we're calling it now?'* I thought to myself. I was on high alert when I pulled up. I had not really been to a man's place, well... for quite some time, and certainly not this early into hanging out.

Deep breaths.

He had a wreath on his door. *Huh... how about that?*

The door burst open and there he was, just beaming at me. And, sure enough, he was getting the water going for tea. *Huh - how about that?*

He had lots of photos framed and hung on the walls - large photo montages with *'Family'* or something printed on the frame. He had a Live, Laugh, Love candle burner in his bathroom. I followed him into the kitchen. The table was pushed off to the side to make room for the gymnastics bar he had set up for his daughter. In the middle of his table was a tile with BE printed in the middle, and other words painted around the side 'be present, be grateful, be happy etc'. He had a photo printed on canvas of the University of Utah football stadium and a few rugby balls. But otherwise, it was pretty darned homey. And clean.

I remember being surprised at the amount of decor a single/ divorced man had in the first place. Initially I thought it was just for the girls. But I was wrong. Jer would have had home decor for himself - the girls just gave him someone to share it with.

Above his patio door in the kitchen was a Christmas decoration that said "MERRY and BRIGHT." This was mid- November, and I didn't see any other Christmas decor out just yet (oh don't worry, I soon would!)

I commented "Getting a jump start on Christmas?"

"Oh no, I like that one - I always have it out." *Huh.... did not see that coming - what is he a big cheese ball?*

He whistled as he watched the water and got out the mugs. *Huh... merry and bright indeed,* he took out a Clorox wipe and wiped down the counter.

After plopping the Sleepy Time bags in the water, we went into the living room and sat down, sipping our tea and just talking.

Jer told me about his life after divorce, how he wanted his life to be, how he wanted to live. He ran out and bought a bunch of nice furniture, and clothing for his new chapter as a single guy, but quickly settled into hanging with his girls. He told me about the dates he'd been on, women who came on too strong, who invited themselves over (even offering to set up their pack-n-plays in the corner to toss their babies in while they....). And how put off he was by it.

I thought it all sounded daunting - trying to create a life different from what you imagined it would be. He and I both had marriages that lasted roughly 15 years, give or take. Jer was empathetic when I explained my situation - a case of two good people who just didn't make a good couple. "Suddenly there's so much water under the bridge and so many old patterns," I trailed off. He nodded in full understanding.

I went over to his place here and there for about a month and each time we sipped tea, and chatted. I told my friend, 'Jeramy invited me over for tea.' 'Oh is that what we're calling it now?' she quipped. "HA! I thought the same thing!" But it's true, we just drank tea and talked.

Thanksgiving was upon us. I assumed, being a single guy that he was like me and took the rolls or maybe the Stovetop stuffing to the family feast. Not Jer. He made a butternut squash cobbler thing with a buttery, vanilla wafer crust. I sat there as he bustled around with cooking the squash, scraping it out, and whatever the other steps were. It was involved. I just sat there and kept him company.

When I stood up to leave, he put a lid on one of the pans and sent me out the door with it. "You want me to take this? What about your family?"

"I made two - one for them, one for you." *What the hell? What am supposed to do with a 9x13 pan of butternut squash cobbler?!* At this point, no one knew he existed. No one at work, certainly not my family. Besides who takes a yam-type of Thanksgiving side-dish into work anyway? There's no way I could bring it back to my mom's (remember I still lived there).

"Well that's sweet of you, thank you."

It pains me to admit I hauled it into work and, when no one was around, I scraped the cobbler into the garbage can. (My dearest love, I'm so, so sorry). I just... I didn't know what else to do with it and a 9x13 is awfully big and my mom would ask questions and so would my coworkers and I just wasn't sure ... and.... and.... I know... shameful.

If it helps your outrage, I'd go on to learn that the butternut dish was one he was known for. His family demanded it every year. They'd call it yams or sweet potatoes and Jer would get all outraged (jokingly of course). It was a favorite. I never, ever told him about that first pan he made me. This is the first time I've come clean. I'd go on to eat many helpings and it's a dish I miss each year. Wish I could scoop it out of the garbage can.

A couple of weeks later, Jer asked me out and in my hesitancy to have any type of relationship I hemmed and hawed a bit, had plans etc. He persisted, "Let's just meet for drinks before my company Christmas thing."

I met him for drinks at a local bar. *Just one glass, I'll have one glass of wine.* I wore a sparkly, mesh sweater with a camisole underneath. I'd worn it to work, I wasn't trying to be racy. He was there waiting for me when I walked in. Sitting in the glow of all the neon and TVs, he beamed at me, got up, gave me a hug, took my coat and helped me sit.

As we sipped our drinks (wine for me, beer for him) he told me how pretty I looked. "Is that your skin?!?" he blurted when he noticed the mesh sweater. "Ha umm... (I looked down) yea?" He smiled and sipped his beer. He was this wonderful combination of grown man with little elements of boyish exuberance that would burst to the surface.

He had to go to his party and I was acting like I had places to be too. He invited me back to his place after, "I don't have to stay at this work thing that long. I'll be home in a little over an hour."

"Well... I'll have to see," I said lying. "I'm getting together with friends and I'll just have to see."

Two drinks later, we went our separate ways. I didn't want to go home. I wasn't sure if I wanted to go to his place - seeing him twice in one night. *Is that like a boyfriend?* Which I desperately did not want. I just, I hadn't yet dated anyone and I was sure I needed to see what, or who, else was out there before I ended up as a couple again.

I went to the mall. I bought a few things. I kept checking for a text. I kept trying to decide if it was okay to go over. I kept trying to figure out what I'd say so that he'd believe all my nonsense. Was it okay to see him again? Twice in the same night?

Finally deciding it was okay, I got take-out from the food court and went back over. He was delighted. He was always delighted. He made tea, he made chocolate chip cookies from scratch, his specialty.

My desire to not end up with a boyfriend, put me on a couple of random dates with other men during the getting-to-know-you phase with Jeramy.

One such date was with an old college friend. Someone I'd dated here and there, maybe kissed once or twice but not much else.

There we were, sharing drinks and dinner. Then more drinks, then more drinks for him. At one point he decided we should go to the neighborhood bar and meet up with his friends. So off we went. The night wore on, later and later. His drinks kept coming long after I'd lost any appetite for mine. His friends were loud and obnoxious, he was drunk and was my ride home.

Finally, his friend making whatever point he was making, began air-boxing… My face. Taking quick jabs toward my face in some type of effort to, well I'm not sure what. This drunk absurdity was the last straw and I told my date I was leaving.

Once locked in my own car, I checked my phone. There was a voicemail from Jeramy "Hey it's me just checking in. I'm not sure what you're up to tonight but if you're around and don't have anything going on, I'm just home doing laundry. I'd love to see you - of course I always love to see you."

I slumped in my car and fought back tears. What on earth was I doing? Why was I trying so hard not to let this guy in? He's home doing laundry and not afraid to say so. He's not out getting drunk. He's not letting his friends air-box my face. What on earth was I doing?

I started to warm up to the idea of having him around. I went over the next night and there he was, sitting on his living room floor putting hand-dipped, chocolate-covered pretzels in Christmasy cellophane bags for his coworkers. *What man does that?*

I plopped down next to him and helped curl the ribbon.

We sat on the floor, side by side. I asked him what it was like telling his daughter that he and his wife were divorcing. Since I was facing the same conversation with my own daughter, I found it helpful, and comforting.

He'd been divorced longer than I had - what was it? Seven years or so. I'd only been separated for two years maybe officially divorced for one, and while that felt plenty long, I hadn't yet dealt with a lot of it - like what to tell Victoria.

She and I had been living at my parents house for those two years and while it was all fun and games at first, she was starting to get pretty pointed in asking why we were living there and when we were going to go home.

As a public relations professional, I was chagrined to realize I'd made the biggest rookie mistake of them all - I didn't control my message. I didn't get out in front of it with my talking points. I was trying to avoid the topic, hoping it would go away. It didn't.

"You're just going to have to tell her," he told me. "The confusion is harder for her than the information." He assured me she'd be fine. He was certain she and I could survive it. This would not the first time that Jeramy knew just what my kid needed.

While my day job was working at Utah's Hogle Zoo in the marketing department, I also freelanced for the local newspaper covering theater in Salt Lake City, which was the job I had prior to switching to the zoo. I invited Jer to join me for a production which he willingly accepted. Still trying to keep a boyfriend at bay, I met friends for dinner and drinks prior and had Jeramy meet me at the theater.

He got there before I did and was waiting for me outside. I texted that I'd be there in three seconds. As soon as he spotted me he held his fingers out in a three-second countdown. It made me chuckle. He wrapped me up in a big Jer hug, kissed my cheek and told me how happy he was to be there.

I remember sitting next to him in the dark theater, feeling his presence, wondering if he'd hold my hand or put his arm around me. I guess I was liking him. Finally, in the last 10 minutes of the show, he reached out rather effortlessly and held my hand. The weight of his arm and the warmth sent a shot through me. *Why on earth did he wait so long?*

I gave him a ride back to his car as we chatted about the show (not our favorite). Pulling up behind his car, I shifted to park. Jer leaned over and gave me one sweet kiss - our first kiss. He didn't hem and haw, he just did it, flashed me a smile and said goodbye.

I drove away smiling.

I'm going to end up with a boyfriend.

THE HOLIDAYS

Jeramy asked me early on about New Year's Eve plans. I didn't know it at the time but Christmas Eve had been a turning point for him; He didn't have his girls that night and as he hung out with a few friends he just missed me. He said it wasn't just a general loneliness, he was lonely for *me* and wanted *me* there; he didn't want to spend another holiday without *me*.

But I didn't know all of that yet. So, he asked about New Year's, he wanted to ring in the new year together. I delayed a bit. I wondered if it'd be better to find something else to do - something that didn't seem to relationshippy. Plus I worked; the Zoo did an early countdown to 9 p.m. to wrap up its ZooLights event. After working outside in the dark cold of Salt Lake City, I never felt like going out afterward.

He was persistent. I told him, "But I work until nine and it's so cold and I can't bear the thought of getting dolled and putting on a cocktail dress."

"I don't want to go out either. I'll cook for you. Just come over, bring a change of clothes and come over as soon as you can."

I told all of my friends, those who now knew he existed, that Costco was going to cook for me.

Half way through my frigid ZooLights shift, Jeramy called me. "Hey, I got out of work late, I think… I think I'm not going to be able to cook tonight. Things are closing and I'm just beat - we had people call out. Do you mind picking up a pizza on your way over?"

WHAT?!?!

I was so annoyed! I looked forward to the dinner, the smells, the warmth, the thought and effort, mostly. I guess you could say, 'I was triggered.' I'd been the only one making an effort before and I wasn't interested in another one of those. I'd done the leg work, I'd done the stopping-on-the-way-home. I was… well.. Triggered.

I fumed to my coworkers who tried to redirect my annoyance. But as I left the Zoo, driving to the damn take n' bake, picturing him warm at home, I was upset.

They were closed. At this point it was 9:30 p.m., I was frozen to the core and there would be no dinner as things were closing - hours ago. I called Jeramy, he didn't answer. I tried again, no answer. I left a voicemail trying not to sound too upset - benefit of the doubt and all.

I got to his house, took a deep breath, closed my eyes and bam - the door was open and there he was - arms outstretched, smile as wide as his wingspan, welcoming me in to warm me up. A big hug, a big kiss and one of those rub the hands up and down the arms for warmth.

My angst began to melt away as he opened up the party hats and glow-in-the-dark necklaces and earrings/bracelets he'd picked up. Pizza was on the way (he'd gotten my message and solved the problem) and just…. He was there. He did put thought into it. He did put in effort - lots of it. He apologized for the change in plans. He was still new in his role managing a Wendy's, so having several employees call out sick threw him on his heels for the evening. Knowing Jeramy now, he must have had a *hell* of a day for him to simplify rather than amplify effort. It must've been brutal. Yet there he was putting on glow in the dark earrings.

The night was perfect. We ate pizza we took our first selfie. He put on some music and we danced in the kitchen - a pretty decent swing step except for one beat, the one after the turn. He'd either add a beat or subtract one but we'd end up on the wrong beat and laugh. He blamed it on me and I blamed it on him (it really was his fault). We watched the ball drop, kissed, and toasted to the new year.

The next morning I texted my friend: My New Year's Eve in emojis: Pizza, wine, music notes, party hats, dancing, smooching and a big, ol' beaming smile. She responded "All of your favorite things!"

It likely goes without saying that Jeramy was growing on me in true Jeramy fashion. He was making sure of that. There were a few Sundays, Jeramy came to our church and found Goldie in the parking lot. One time he just left a note saying how much fun he had the night before. Another Sunday he left me a container of chocolate chip cookies sitting on top of the van with a sweet note. I sat there reading the note thinking *'he was here?? He came all the way out here??'* I looked around and of course he was gone.

I decided to make my first stop at his Wendy's one Sunday after church. I figured Victoria wouldn't really pay too much attention and a quick stop through the drive thru couldn't be that big of a deal, could it?

Pulling up to the menu board I recognized his voice "Welcome to Wendy's can I take your order?"

"Yea, I'll have a large unsweet iced tea please."

"I'D KNOW THAT VOICE ANYWHERE!" he said in an exuberant British accent. I immediately appreciated this reference to Mary Poppins (when Bert sees Mary's silhouette on the sidewalk) and pulled around to get my drink - for free - plus a Frosty for Victoria.

A few weeks later, he left a note that said he'd like to see me Wednesday and Thursday nights. Those were my two weeknights without Victoria. I asked him 'You want to see me this Wednesday and Thursday night or every Wednesday and Thursday night?" "YES!"

We discovered The Westerner, our local country western bar, offered free country swing dance lessons on Thursday nights so we started going to those and refused to switch partners when instructed to do so. We (he) never totally figured out that one beat.

Naturally we had a date for Valentine's Day. Also, by this point, I'd told my mom he existed. Side note - she already knew something was up and wasn't at all surprised. What is it with moms anyway? Can never pull anything over on them.

I got a picture text from him of a bouquet of flowers sitting in the Costco service area with an envelope taped to it that read "Mi Hermosa." I chuckled - someone has the same nickname as me, how about that? I didn't think another thing of it.

Then a text message - "Man the Zoo is busy today."

Then another picture text of a little gift with balloons sitting on the table at the pizza place where we had our first date. It was just a picture of the gift on the table "Pizza sounds good today!!!"

I responded "HA! Wait... what? Is that our pizza place? And you were at the Zoo? What are you up to?"

He responded with a picture text of a bag of goodies and balloons wrapped around a light pole in the parking lot of The Westerner. I was busy with my day, and knew we had plans that night. I found the texts charming but a bit confusing.

More texts:

J - Have you already collected your things?

Me - *collected my things???* No - I haven't had a chance! *Scrambling here*.... I thought you'd come with me.

J - Oh cool OK

Me - Or should I go first? *I haven't showered yet!* Either way... I wasn't sure...

J - That's entirely up to you! It's for you!

Me - (Realizing he'd created a scavenger hunt all over town and it was completely lost on me) So they're all waiting for me?? At The Westerner, pizza place and Costco? ... Really?...

J- Yup

Me - Oh my gosh.... HA!!!!!

J - Costco first, Zoo, pizza, Westerner

Me - Oh my hell... What am I going to do with you?... K, I'll be in touch!

J - Haha we can go together if you want

Talk about just not picking up on any hints. For the geography of SLC, all of the places were 20-30 minutes apart, depending on traffic. I just didn't know. I'd never had a scavenger hunt. I hadn't showered yet, I was planning to gussy up for our date that night.

We ended up driving around together to pick up my gifts - all over the valley. We stopped at the zoo after it had closed and had the place to ourselves. When people used to ask me the best times to visit the zoo, I'd quip - "before we open and after we close." It's such a treat to hear the animals, but also to hear the quiet. Most folks don't get to experience that. The freeroaming peacocks strutted around like working stiffs who'd just clocked out. The seals and sea lions paid us no mind and neither did the Amur tiger, deliberately surveying his habitat, deciding where to finally lie down. It was a balmy night, for February. We strolled through the Zoo and took a sunset selfie. We chuckled at how I *completely* missed the clues. Completely. I felt bad as it took extraordinary effort on his part, but Jer was amused by it.

Later that night, as he drove me back to my car, he pulled up a song on his playlist and played "Come to Me" by The Goo

Goo Dolls - a band I was completely unfamiliar with. But the Universe, in all its vastness, speaks to me through music. Always has.

SONGBIRD

My folks often quip that I came out singing - that I could sing before I could talk. It was actually my kindergarten teacher who pulled my mom aside and said "you need to get her in singing, she's a little songbird." Mrs. Abegglen paid attention to my endless enthusiasm during singing time and my mom listened to her.

I took piano lessons for years and eventually added voice lessons. I performed in a singing/ performing group in my youth and sang in choirs my whole life - through elementary, jr high, high school and into college. I sang a season or two with the Utah Symphony Chorus as well. Our high school musicals were 'Oklahoma," "Camelot," and "My Fair Lady" - I was a singing maid.

At that same time, I worked retail in the local mall. One of my coworkers was a gal named Amy. She was about a foot shorter than I - came up to my collarbone - and packed so much personality into that frame. Amy wore bright red lipstick, giant earrings and was from Baltimore (pronounced "Bol-ti-Moah" in her wonderful east coast accent).

While I grew up watching the old school musicals, Amy introduced me to current Broadway. It sounds silly to say, but

I didn't realize Broadway was still going on. This was before the internet and how would a gal from Salt Lake know about mythical Broadway? Amy made me a mix tape of songs - "Miss Saigon," "Aspects of Love," "Chess."

I devoured "Phantom of the Opera," next was "Les Miserables."

I'm sure I owe my family an apology as I'd walk around the house with my ghetto blaster playing my mix tape, playing "Phantom," singing along - always singing along. (I actually owe them an apology for my high school production of "Camelot" as well - Subject matter beyond the scope of high schoolers, clocking in at three hours long).

Once I got into college, it was tricky to find the time to commit to performing. I was taking a full college course load and working full time (not the ideal college experience) so I took a break from the stage. But I never took a break from discovering new music.

When I say the Universe speaks to me through music, I mean it. And I say Universe meaning God, energies, guides, angels, whatever you subscribe to. I just think Universe sounds as vast as all of the varied philosophies, so I tend to settle on that term.

There are two moments in my life I can use as an example of the power of music to my soul:

One being when I was eight months pregnant with Victoria. I had recently lost my job as a morning radio host. I also lost the show I hosted on Saturday nights, my beloved Showtune Saturday Night. I was absolutely distraught. We pulled out of the house offered we'd made. I had nothing to do during the days except sit around and wonder what on earth life had in store for me, who's going to hire a very pregnant chick and why on earth did we decide to have a kid?!

My brain booted up a song for me that I hadn't listened to since the Broadway mix tape Amy made for me while I was back in high school, "The Sacred Bird," from Miss Saigon.

"...I am happy today, for I know what to do,

And my heart is not torn."

Being the musical theater nerd I am, I'm aware that the mother in this moment is contemplating the unimaginable. But before she does, she sings this line:

"I know now why I came to this earth, it's so you find your place."

In the final weeks leading up to the birth of my soul-reason for existing, my exquisite Victoria, I sang that line over and over and over. I had that song on repeat and I'd sing up through that line and start the song again. It was as though God was saying 'you have a bigger purpose than hosting a radio show. There is more for you, I promise.' And, being omnipotent, He knew He had to sing it to me in order for me to hear it.

Victoria would burst into this world in a fury, via last-minute C-section (her wails heard through two sets of hospital doors by her eager grandparents waiting out in the hallway). It would be two hours before I got to see her or hold her.

They placed her in my arms and I burst into the most uncontrollable, joyous tears, as I looked as this beautiful, sleeping creature. I had never seen anything like it. Nothing so delicate, nothing so pure, nothing so beautiful - I wept.

Victoria, all bundled up, still hadn't opened her eyes; she was so peaceful. I knew nothing about being a mother, but I did know you didn't want to wake a sleeping baby. So I just held her and looked at her.

After about an hour, I began to sing - "I know now why I came to this earth.." softly; to myself, to my sleeping baby. "...It's so you find your place." In that moment Victoria, still fast asleep, flashed opened those eyes and looked directly into mine. I wept again. "I know now why I came to this earth," I sang that line again. "...It's so you find your place."

She looked at me so intently. As though she was thinking 'I know you! THAT'S where that song comes from. I know that song. I know that voice. I know you."

My second example of music's presence was several months later. Victoria was still a baby - I'm not sure how old. I was struggling. My husband and I worked opposite shifts so we didn't have to put Victoria in daycare. So I'd bail out early for work (that was my newspaper job) and I'd get home at 1 p.m. My husband would leave at 1:30 p.m. and work until 11 or later. I was home alone with Victoria every night and it was grueling. I didn't know what I was doing. I didn't have any friends with kids that age and I just felt very alone.

The Universe, knowing I needed a lifeline, sent me the song "I Get to Show you the Ocean," by Georgia Stitt (sung beautifully by Faith Prince). It was about a mom introducing the world to her child -

"I'm gonna show you ocean

You're gonna play in the sand.

You've never been to the ocean, or stood on the turf where the surf meets the land.

I get to show you the ocean, your eyes will widen with glee

You'll watch the fishies that tan in the tide pools, I'll watch my love fall in love with the sea."

I played that song over and over and was finally able to take a deep breath; those words helped me shift my perspective. It was going to be okay. My life was going to be okay. And I'd get to introduce my daughter to the ocean, and the world.

So there we were. Our Valentine's scavenger hunt items all gathered and Jer singing along to his playlist.

"I'll be kind, if you'll be faithful

You be sweet and I'll be grateful…."

He wasn't just singing along - he was singing TO me.

"….And when we're old and near the end,

We'll go home and start again."

I mean, he was cute, no doubt, but I was also pretty sure there was no way he knew what he was singing. In my experience, men typically listened to music for the beat, the riffs and the vibe, they basically never listened to the words; to the message of the song.

"I caught you burnin' photographs

Like that could save you from your past.

History's like gravity

It holds you down away from me.

You and me, we've both got sins

And I don't care about where you've been.

Don't be sad and don't explain

This is where we start again…

Start again…."

Huh… I thought to myself… I wonder if he knows he's basically saying he doesn't need all the details of what happened in my marriage. He doesn't care about any moments I wasn't proud of. I mean… the song is basically saying to let that stuff go and just start fresh. I wonder if he knows that's what he's singing to me?"

"Today's the day I make you mine

THE HOPE AT THE END OF THE TUNNEL

So get me to the church on time.

Take my hand in this empty room

You're my girl and I'm your groom.

Come to me my sweetest friend, this is where we start again.."

How cute. He's singing about marriage and doesn't even know it.

WRITING OUR STORY

(Written 3/7/15, after a practically perfect day)

He told me he loved me today. Not today really, two days ago. Two days ago, at the end of a rough day, he grabbed me by my arms with a glint in his eye and said "I'm pretty sure I'm so freaking in love with you I don't even know what to do." Of course I didn't say anything, I rarely do - not because I don't want to but because I don't know how. The words get stuck in my throat. But he meant it. And I felt it.

I wasn't entirely surprised, only because this man says what he thinks and, at least to my eye, can't entirely hide what he's feeling. So for a while, I'd been thinking 'he wants to tell me he loves me but is unsure about my reaction.'

But today, with my feet in his lap, and the first gin and tonic of the season in my hand, the sun baking our winter-weary souls, I leaned forward while fighting back tears and told him the same.

I too had been thinking it for a while, I mean, watching him bake, watching his animation while telling stories, sensing his warmth, seeing him offer his hand, his exuberance, his support with my upcoming move, his unwavering willingness to express his feelings. I knew that he could see it (he does that sort of thing). But I was trying to fight it, like I do.

YYet today, I watched him rifle through his tool chest to fix the blinker on my car (an annoying task). He whistled, he had a spring in his step, he just… helped me. But more importantly, he seemed to want to; slightly foreign to me.

We drove to Orem. We sang "Annie." We analyzed the lyrics. We learned about mickey fins and Don Budge - both referenced in the musical.

We ate Thin Mints and ate too much at Wendy's. The day was full of light and warmth and the weather was beautiful too. We stopped for tonic, limes and gin.

And, as usual, he opened up. We talked and laughed and shared and had a truly beautiful conversation about life, the past and the bright looking future.

Then, with warmth in our hearts, we painted. We went to a wine and paint mixer and painted red wine being poured into a goblet.

One wine glass was beautifully curved on top, sexy, smooth. The other was slightly lopsided, bulbous on the underside, mostly Picasso-esque but full of life and movement.

Moments were clunky. Moments were a bit drunken but, blended with our classmates, we painted. We painted movement. We painted low-lights but more importantly we painted highlights. Brushes dipped in white paint carefully - with a steady hand - lightly tracing the delicate curve of the glass.

I marveled at his decisiveness, his direction, his ability to anticipate the instruction and just charge ahead and do what felt right.

It's an example, really, for his approach to life.

And I like that.

Rather, I think I love it.

JOLLY HOLIDAY

Victoria and I went out looking for new apartments. We zeroed in on one that was only 15 minutes from my folks'. A townhome style, two-story, two-bed apartment with a garage. The front window looked out at the playground and there were already kids out there playing. It would be perfect.

I got the keys and that night Jeramy picked me up so we could go take a look. We stopped for burritos. He'd brought a box with a blanket, paper towels, utensils - all the things we'd need for a picnic on the floor.

For my housewarming gift, he gave me a stainless steel garbage can with a lid; still serving me well over there against the wall, under the Merry and Bright sign. He wrote the nicest note about things that happened in the past, should be taken out with the trash. It's time to begin a new life with a fresh start.

He had a hard time not being able to help us move in. Victoria hadn't met him yet, he worked that day and there was a lot going on. He wasn't happy about it, I kept telling him it was fine, but he didn't like it. He did have pizza sent over that night so that we'd have something to eat.

The move-in process had just begun and I had to leave town for a work conference. I'd be gone five days and while we hated being apart, he said he'd keep himself busy.

Zoo conferences can be a bit of a whirlwind with workshops during the day, ice breakers and socializing at night and sometimes more drinks with colleagues after we had broken the ice. I checked in with Jer regularly but it proved to be a long week.

The night before I was to fly home, he and I missed one another for FaceTime, I missed a second call and finally texted him that I was heading to bed. It was a bit early for bedtime but I was exhausted and not interested in anymore drinking or hanging out.

Since the Zoo is a non-profit, we had to share rooms when we traveled. My roommate and I were all tucked in bed, done for the day and Jeramy called. I didn't want to disrupt my roommate *is she asleep?* So I ignored the call, figuring I'd already told him I was heading to bed.

I laid there in the dark room seeing that he was calling again. I think I texted that I couldn't talk. I don't remember what he texted back but I got a clear message that he did not like what was happening.

I felt annoyed for a second until I took a breath and connected a few dots. We'd been communicating regularly and he's had no problem with my going out and enjoying the conference. I randomly 'went to bed early,' missing his call and he has no idea why or where I am or any of it. I'd be bugged too. Also, why was I more concerned about my roommate than my sweetheart?

I got out of bed, slipped on a hoodie and whispered 'I need to go make a call.' Naturally, roomie didn't care and it was none of her business anyway.

I was freezing but I went and stood in the stairwell and FaceTimed this wonderful man so he could see that in fact, I had turned in early, I was all finished with the day and looking forward to seeing him tomorrow.

The FaceTime connected and there he was, standing in my new kitchen looking slightly distraught but so relieved to see me. He was right, he had been keeping himself busy. He showed me a cleaned kitchen, with our wine glass paintings up above the cabinets. He bought me cleaning supplies, hung a rack in the garage where I could hang mops and brooms. He'd washed and cleaned Goldie, organized the garage. He been tirelessly making my chaotic new apartment a home.

He was so relieved to see me freezing in the stairwell, make-up removed, hair pulled up. He talked about how he felt like a jackass that he was home doing all this work while picturing me out on the town. "I just got in my head," he said. "That's why I wanted you to see me," I replied. "I want you to know you can trust me, I'm right here and I can't wait to see you tomorrow." He looked 100 pounds lighter and told me to get out of the stairwell and let him know when I was safe, back in my room.

I laid there smiling. I made the right decision. It was worth getting up, getting cold and bothering my roommate. I brought him peace of mind and he was worth that.

When my plane touched down and I walked toward baggage claim, there he was, my sweetheart, standing inside waiting for me. You might be thinking 'huh... just standing there? That doesn't sound like Jer' and you would be right. He stood there with eight helium balloons, all colors of the rainbow, a black and white polka-dotted bag full of treats and snacks and a large fluorescent pink poster board that read "Welcome Home Mi Hermosa!"

I thought the effort was because we had that misunderstanding but that wasn't it at all. That's how Jeramy picks up his love from the airport - always inside, and always with a extra something - flowers, signs, treats, you name it. One sign read "I AM SO IN LOVE WITH THIS WOMAN!' Ha! So many people enjoyed watching him, waiting to see who this mystery woman was. Then it was me. I told him they're going to wonder what's wrong with you - but, just like you'd imagine, Jeramy didn't care.

We took our first road trip together up to Idaho, about a five hour drive. He was playing in a racquetball tournament. The year before, he and his teammates all brought their kids and stayed in some type of Holidome place - they had a ball. Even without the kids this year, he knew we'd have fun.

We spent every spare second together but I was getting anxious that this is a lot of time together. A lot. What if he grows tired of me? What if I run out of things to say? What if I say too much? What if, what if? None of that ever occurred to him (naturally) and off we went.

We went up on a Friday and had time to kill. We roamed around the little main street looking in shops. I remember the sun shining, only needing a jacket, holding hands, laughing and it was just…. nice.

Jer heartily greeted all the shop keepers, told them about the tournament. He heartily greeted everyone we passed. We chuckled at seeing Mary Poppins and Bert on the other side of the street, dressed in costume, passing out flyers for their upcoming production of the stage version of "Mary Poppins." He bought me a pair of earrings, he bought me a cup of coffee.

We always chuckled getting coffee as Jer would get the biggest macchiato-frappucino-sugary-latte-with-cream thing they could make and I would just get coffee with a bit of cream. They'd always hand me his drink and hand him mine.

As we stopped to fix my coffee, Jer saw the performers coming into the coffee shop. The sun was low in the sky, casting sun patches and shadows inside. As soon as they walked in, Jer burst out "I'd know that silhouette anywhere!" - one of Bert's lines from the movie.

The performers looked a bit startled, trying to stay in character, they tried ad-libbing with Jer who could basically out-adlib anyone at any time. By the time this impromptu exchange was over, Bert huddled close to Jer, dropped his accent, stepped out of character and said "Seriously, how'd you know that line? That's seriously one of my lines - Have you played Bert before?" "Well… it's in the movie?…" Jer responded a bit bewildered. Naturally, a photo was in order to commemorate our jolly holiday.

Jer didn't win the tourney but I loved watching him play. He was good, he was lighthearted, everyone loved him. I worried they'd wonder what he saw in me - he was just so…. fun.

I had to be back home to get Victoria and it was Easter Sunday. Jer offered to help. He dropped me off, ran to the store and picked up *all* the Easter treats and trinkets - far more than I ever would have bought. She hadn't met him yet, but she was already falling in love with him too.

PATSY CLINE

My folks often had the country music station on in the car and I always liked it; just as much as the pop music of the day, not that I ever would have admitted that to any of my friends. I ejected my Judds cassette every time friends got in the car; no one listened to country. But when my folks took me to piano lessons or when they picked me up after school, we listened to country.

My quest for consuming any and all types of music led me to steal my mom's Patsy Cline cassette tape. Patsy Cline's 12 Greatest Hits was one exquisitely-sung, heartbreaking love song after another. No one else sang like that. Her contralto range was also unique and easy for me to sing along with. I hadn't heard notes like that before except maybe Anne Murray, I liked singing with her too; Karen Carpenter maybe?

Anyway, I loved Patsy, I always loved Patsy. Fast forward many years- I was now grown, working as a co-host on a morning FM radio station. The Grand Theater, where I'd performed many times, announced auditions for the show "Always… Patsy Cline," an off-Broadway musical telling the story of a friendship forged between Patsy and a fan she met one night at a honky-tonk in Dallas (based on a true story). It's a two woman show with a live, six-piece band.

Well that threw me into high gear. My husband at the time came to bed one night and said he looked it up and "Always Patsy has 27 songs in it." I felt a jolt of panic/dread/unbridled excitement and oh-shit all at the same time.

27 solos is an extraordinary amount - that's a concert, not a musical. That's a monster role. Even the leads in the most well-known and beloved musicals get four maaaaybe five solos (one of those usually a reprise). I'd never heard of anything like it.

I had an amazing vocal and acting coach I was working with at the time, Victoria Mallory. I'd like to pause long enough to pay my respects to this wonderful human we lost a few years back to pancreatic cancer. She was grace, beauty, talent, warmth, compassion and kindness all wrapped up in a petite frame with shiny black hair and the sparkliest eyes. She was a former Broadway star turned soap opera star and was living in Park City - about a 30 minute drive out of SLC. She generously shared her talent and wisdom and hardly charged anything for it. A remarkable human and was a big inspiration for my daughter's name. I listened to Patsy on my way to my lesson, we worked hard on the material for an hour (she often gave me an extra 30 minutes without charging) and I listened to Patsy on the way home. I relished the drive, the time and the lessons.

We worked on audition songs, I kept getting called back. I did about three or four callbacks. For the last one, I had to sing "Lovesick Blues" - an old Hank Williams tune that Patsy performed with many of her signature growls and yodels. The director, and the music director stepped out of the room to chat and I just stood there waiting, looking around.

I got the part! I remember leaving the callback in a stunned elation. I went to the liquor store to get some champagne and headed over to my folks to celebrate with my built-in cheering section (my siblings still lived there at the time).

Then the real work commenced. All told, Victoria Mallory and I worked on the Patsy catalog for a year from audition to the first performance. I spent more time watching videos of Patsy than most people do bingeing Netflix.

Ms. Mallory not only helped me with the singing but with the performing - how to walk up to a microphone like a star; we worked on the fact that not every song in concert has to end on a button, like in musical theater where the cast strikes a big, smiley pose on the last beat of the song; we figured out where to stick in various Patsy nuances I'd read about or watched.

I worked on my own too. I read biographies, watched documentaries and listened to her music non-stop. I know every breath, every pause, every quiver, every nuance - I just love her. I love the stories I've heard and read, I love how bold and sassy she was, I felt an inexplicable connection with her - still do.

Our show was a huge success! The most popular show at The Grand Theatre at the time, playing to packed houses. Night after night, the audience leapt to their feet, they whistled at the band, they couldn't wait to come find me afterward and tell me how much they loved the show. Patsy is still and will always be the highlight of my performing life.

(I'm actually drinking out of a Patsy Cline coffee mug as I write this). Patsy would not only be the wind in my musical and performing sails for a major chapter in my life, she would bring with her strangers who became the truest kind of friends.

The first time I met Matt Wall was backstage during a dress rehearsal. The show has so many wig and costume changes that two dressers are required. Those dressers meet the Patsy (me) as she exits the stage and help her waltz through something like 12 costume changes and as many wig changes throughout the night.

We had two dressers booked for the run and one backed out so they called Matt. All I knew about him was he had dressed actors at the local professional theater. I turned around to meet him and thought I was meeting a 12 year- old boy. I towered over him - especially in my heels - he seemed unsure, a bit hesitant and this show was too important to me to offer a whole lot of chances.

After we ran the show, the wig master came back chuckling and said "Matt put all the wigs on sideways" meaning Patsy's curls above her ears were in the middle of my forehead like Superman. My stress was high, my frustration was higher. This wasn't going to work.

I pulled the director aside and said "he's not going to work. I think we're going to have to find someone else." I meant it. I'd spent a year of my life on this project, I was already nervous I wouldn't be able to pull it off and I couldn't be distracted by this kid. Lucky for me, the director said "well, let's run it one more time and see how we do."

From that moment on, Matt, Matty Wall as we call him, would take up a spot in my heart and my world and he's still there to this day. Our next run-through was spot-on - so were the wigs. To use a musical term, he didn't miss a beat. I'd come to learn he was fun, he was funny, he worked hard and he wasn't 12 but only four years younger than I was.

When Patsy ended, we met for lunch at a KFC. I was nervous that we'd not have much to talk about without the show but that was NOT a problem at all. We would continue on - sheesh for almost 20 years now - meeting for lunches or dinners (one time he set the menu on fire by accidentally holding it too close to the candle), shopping (one time I accidentally flashed him by spinning in the wrap dress I was trying on), and getting together for take-n-bake pizza and some TV. We've taken dozens of trips together from Jackson Hole to Seattle, from Maui to Puerto Vallarta, and there is not a town where Matty and I haven't had a burrito.

We just hang out, and chat and often chuckle that we might look like an odd pair, we wonder if people think I'm his sugar mama. We people watch - watching for cute boys and giggling cause sometimes we can't figure out 'which one does he like? Which one does he like?'

For four years I wrote for the local newspaper as their theater editor which required me to see and review just about every piece of theater happening in Utah. I loved that job - theater is a passion of mine and the job was a perfect fit. That set us up for our glory years - frequent nights out to various shows from community theater, to Broadway tours, we drove the length of Utah from Logan down to St. George seeing shows.

But a highlight for both of us are the numerous treks to New York City to drink in some Broadway. We've gone in summer, we've gone in the dead middle of winter. We eat cupcakes, we get Nuts4Nuts, we buy umbrellas when the Big Apple sky opens up. We tromped through Times Square when the town shut down for snow, we wiped our sweaty brows in the heat of August standing in the TKTS line or waiting outside for our matinees to begin. We've waited at stage doors and he took a really crappy picture of me with Kristin Chenoweth.

We've seen countless shows on Broadway (actually we should really try to count them), we got fancy and attended the Tony Awards and he was with me when I covered the Tony Awards as a reporter.

When my in-laws at the time wanted me to take my 2 ½ year old daughter for a visit to Maui, I called Matty as I didn't feel experienced enough as a mom to haul a toddler and all of her belongings through an airport and handle the transfers by myself (my husband couldn't get the time off). So Matty came along and was delighted to do so - he helped entertain Victoria, he slept on the kitchen floor on an air mattress without complaint, my in-laws loved him (everyone does). We drove the island, we ate cinnamon rolls on the way to the beach, we ate burritos at the beach.

It's mostly fun and games with us but not always. I was there during Matty's journey to come out to his family, I sang at his grandmother's funeral and have talked him through various heartbreaks and disappointments. Matty was there through the death of my grandparents, my divorce, and my various other heartbreaks - of which there are many.

His calm demeanor, oolness under fire andwit can help diffuse about any situation. Whether he's fixing a broken zipper backstage seconds before an entrance, or engaging with a toddler during flight delays, he's steady, he's present and he's ready to help.

Sadly, my time at the newspaper came to an end (company-wide layoffs). I got a new job doing PR for Hogle Zoo and Matty eventually chased his dreams with a move to L.A.. The only solace is that he returns to SLC often for visits and his work-from-home job allows him to stay a while. To this day, we communicate almost daily swapping hijinks, funny tales, and yes, a heartbreak or two.

We would go on to revive Patsy numerous times over the following 15 years, Matty standing backstage with my wig at pretty much every run. I think he only missed one and we were both distraught about it.

The band and I formed a Patsy tribute band and have played numerous gigs throughout the state, including at the Heber Valley Cowboy Poetry and Music Festival (Matty flew in to help).

People love Patsy's music, there's no doubt. But I think they also feel my personal love for and connection with Patsy. When I sing her music, I feel her so closely. It's almost as if God lets her come visit and walk through a night with me - lending me her essence. While the show, vocally, is a wallop, there are some nights it feels so effortless, it's almost as if I'm not even really singing. I end the show and bow feeling so energized, I'm ready to take it from the top and start all over.

SUMMER DAYS

The Patsy team and I were slated for another revival of "Always... Patsy Cline" that spring, May to be exact. Jer had never seen me perform before and I was excited for him to see the show. He loved musicals and had been listening to Patsy to get to know her songs better. He listened with me but I was even more delighted that he listened on his own as well. It meant a lot - another way he showed his support.

Since we'd done the show three or four times by then, our rehearsals were pretty quick. Each night after rehearsal, Jer would be there asking me how it went. We hadn't really spent any time apart yet so rehearsals felt like a bit of a stretch. One night I knew I was getting finished just after 6 p.m., which meant I could be to his house around 6:30 p.m. I pulled up to his place and could see he set up his balcony for a candle-light dinner. I sat in my car for a moment, looked at the set-up watching him bustle around the kitchen and thought to myself, 'wow I could get used to coming home to this man.'

He had one of those teeny apartment balconies that make no sense - more of a place to take a smoke break than an outdoor space to enjoy - and he had no patio furniture (which wouldn't have fit anyway) but he knew I loved being outside on beautiful nights, and we loved to watch the sun set. He took two TV trays, pushed them together and took his big kitchen chairs out there. We were knee-to-knee and I loved everything about it.

He told everyone he knew about the production and wanted everyone to see it (even before he knew if it was any good). He had people scheduled to see the show with him at every performance.

I told him he might want to see it first by himself, explaining that watching someone perform who you are close to can be quite moving. But he wanted everyone to see it, so he brought people to every show.

"You were right," he said after he saw it. "I should have seen it by myself the first time. I thought I'd start crying."

He loved it.

He sent flowers backstage. He brought his homemade cookies to a matinee for the cast and crew to munch on between shows. He got to meet Matty and I finally introduced him to my parents.

"We liked him instantly," they texted me after they left.

That summer, I had a booking at the Ed Kenley Amphitheater in Layton, Utah. This is a great little venue on a beautiful summer night. It can seat around 1,200 people, many of them seated on blankets and chairs on the grass. Folks can bring in coolers of food and drink and they have a whole season of great music - everything from Air Supply to the Nitty Gritty Dirt Band.

My years with Patsy opened the door to create concert evenings. We did Patsy as a concert, of course. Then we branched out - I did the music of Peggy Lee and an evening of love songs. This summer I was preparing "The Music of the Carpenters, Carole King and Linda Ronstadt."

This was all new material for me (Linda Ronstadt is very difficult to sing!). I also had the idea to feature Victoria in the Carpenters song "Sing." We practiced every time we were in the car together. Jer was involved in the whole preparation for the show and was, of course, our most enthusiastic supporter.

He sent flowers backstage for Victoria and me and sat next to my mom during the show. He also had his whole family come - they sat back on the grass and were among my loudest cheering section.

Victoria got a hearty standing ovation and was the cutest darn thing. She chatted with the crowd saying "I've lost seven teeth and I'm seven and a half and I go to Horizon Elementary."

The show is still a personal highlight for me. I loved the material, I loved that the crowd sang along to every single word of every single song. I loved that they stayed all the way to the end, even though it began raining. I loved singing with my daughter.

Jer met us backstage, got our stuff loaded in the car then met us at home. He had Double Stuffed Oreos ready to share with Victoria and a celebratory wine ready to share with me.

Afterward my mom said she thought Jeramy was just going to burst. The second I walked on stage he was just bursting with pride and excitement and she worried he couldn't contain himself.

The band and I were booked at a few county fairs throughout Utah. Some of these towns were three or more hours away and we all just got ourselves there at whatever time we needed to for set up. Jer happily took over as my personal chauffeur, costume carrier, and sometimes agent. He made sure I had what I needed; made sure I'd gotten my Patsy microphone back in its box and made sure I got safely back home afterward. We listened to Patsy on the way there and talked about how it went on the way home. He listened if I had frustrations; he bought us fries to share if we felt we needed some.

I chuckled once and asked him if he ever thought he'd know as much about Patsy Cline as he did. He laughed and said, "No - but I'm sure glad I do."

COUPLE GOALS

Music stitched itself throughout the rest of our summer as well. We did some 'family outings' to the weekly Big Band Night in downtown Salt Lake City - free performances at the Gallivan Center. We loved it. We brought our blankets, listened to the jazz standards and tried to figure out that swing step from time to time.

We all had rousing sing-along concerts in the car to "Jekyll + Hyde," the new album by Zac Brown Band. I'd been a long time ZBB fan. Jer was fully on board with becoming a fan as well and the girls weren't far behind. He cranked the volume and we all sang along.

In an unusual match-up, ZBB partnered with Sara Bareilles on a delightful duet called "Mango Tree." It's this big band tune that swings right out of the speakers, standing out against the rest of the southern country/rock songs on the album.

Naturally, we became terrific duet partners. Jer took Zac's part and I'd come in where Sara did. Every time I made my entrance, Jer would burst into the biggest grin, "there she is!" and he patted his heart as though it was going to beat right out of his ches. (Jer an I would later work up some choreography and perform Mango Tree for his family during their little Christmas Eve family talent show - typically reserved for the kids to play piano and such - but we were fantastic!)

We trekked off to numerous concerts that year - from ZBB, to Broadway star Brian Stokes Mitchell; from Garth Brooks; to the Utah Symphony's summer concert series on the hillside of the beautiful Deer Valley ski resort.

It's funny, thinking back, I'm struck by the fact that most people knew Jer to be a rocker (AC/DC, Van Halen) but I don't see him that way. He always listened to what I wanted to - happily - from Broadway to Patsy. I have zero memory of listening to Van Halen with him - which I guess makes me sad.

I loved our non-kid weekends but I equally loved our weekends with the girls. I loved watching him dote on each one - including Victoria. We did swimming nights at my apartment pool. We tried grilling a pizza and Jer nearly caught the apartment on fire. He did whale breeches in the pool for the kids. We did family nights in the hot tub. We took some road trips down to Southern Utah. We got to know each other's families. He wrote and left love notes everywhere (he did that until the day he died) "I love you a LOT!" "You're so sexy," "I love you. I can't wait to see you!" He made countless batches of cookies, we had nights with wine and conversation (we didn't even own a TV for the longest time), foot rubs and so much laughter.

Jer's daughter said she could picture us in "old people chairs." We had our own jokes, we were creating something new - something that felt as sure as anything - I actually never doubted it.

One day, we were all chatting and laughing about what Jer's white Nissan should be named and, without skipping a beat, his oldest daughter came up with Betty White - the perfect match for Goldie. It stuck. Sometimes she'd go by "Betts" as well.

We also had a big, in-depth discussion about "XOXO." We were trying to figure out how that came to represent hugs and kisses. We felt like the O should be the hug, the shape your arms make when they wrap around someone. And the X should be for kisses kind of like the crinkles in your lips when you pucker. Hence, OXOX was adopted by our family and that's how we always signed things - with OXOX.

Jeramy was named general manager for a brand new Wendy's. His goal was to work up to be a regional manager, checking in on restaurants and helping them meet their goals. His Wendy's became a homebase for our whole crew. Anyone could stop in there, be greeted with a big Jer hug, receive food (for free even though that was never our intention). When I'd stop in, his employees would all start smiling waiting for him to notice. Or they'd say "Hefeeeeeeeee" (which is really 'jefe' - Spanish for boss). He'd turn and see me and bellow something like "Mi Hermosa Donette!" or "There's the most beautiful woman in the world!" and when I say bellow, I mean it - he shouted out for the whole restaurant to hear. He'd ring up my order with a smirk on his face and never charge me. When my order was ready, his employees would get on the microphone and call out "most beautiful" or whatever name Jer entered in for my order. Sometimes they couldn't bring themselves to do it. They got on the mic, before they were paying attention, look at the name, panic and just say "Umm... you" when they caught my eye. Sometimes they just walked the meal out to me, rather than have to call out some embarrassing name for the whole restaurant.

Jer was usually too busy to stop and chat much, but I didn't mind. I had to eat lunch anyway and I loved watching him work. I know the above interactions sound like he just treated me that way but that's not the case. Aside from the lovey-dovey pet names, he greeted every customer with the same warmth. He knew them by name, he knew their orders. He took selfies with them. He had nicknames for them. Some would come up to me and say 'He's the whole reason I come in here,' and I'd say 'Me too.'

Sometimes Jer would get a feeling or vibe from customers in the drive-thru. He'd pause long enough to ask them how they were doing that day, genuinely. He'd toss in something extra for free, he tried to make them smile. He often ended up causing a few tears of joy.

If that's how he treated his customers, you can imagine how he was with his employees. They adored him, they loved his warmth, his flexibility with their schedules, his understanding that they had families, sometimes multiple jobs, one or no cars. He cared about them as people and they worked hard for him. He led some employees through their first jobs and created shift leaders and managers out of others.

When we were out together, people were envious of us and I loved that. We often had people come up to us an say "You guys are so cute" "You guys are couple goals" - often. I'd never had that before. It was all Jer - it was the way he paid attention, it was how damn happy he always seemed just to be sitting there participating.

Everything was more fun with Jer around. Just little things. Randomly adding McDonald's french fries to our drink order. Tossing a cheap toy into the shopping cart when Victoria asked, Oreo nights, practicing harmonies in the car, decorating for Valentine's Day.

My sister recalls a random night in January where we'd sent her a picture text of us wearing a sombreros, holding maracas. I had to tell her it was our Mexican escape that night, complete with margaritas and guacamole. I mean what else would you be doing on a Wednesday night in January?

Every time I came home to him, I knew I was right, I loved coming home to him. He'd greet me at the door, he'd take my bags, hug and kiss me. He'd have dinner, he'd have a joke, he'd tell me how glad he was that I was back. Sometimes, if I was going to beat him home, he'd leave me welcome home notes. Or, he'd have wine poured with a sticky note that said "Here you go, can't wait to join you." Sometimes I'd come home to nothing but candle light. Jer was not a gourmet chef but he could certainly throw a meal together and he added all these little touches like the candles or cloth napkins from time to time and I felt completely spoiled.

We continued for the most blissful year and half I've ever experienced. Nothing but joy. He loved my family, they loved him. We loved his family, they loved us. We did things - everything and nothing. It was pure contentment with great excitement thrown in.

TOGETHER AT LAST

By 2016, the Broadway musical "Hamilton" was all the rage and I needed to be a part of it, so, we took a trip to New York City. Broadway was new for Jer but I have made it a mission to get to NYC as often as time and budgets allow, cramming in as many musicals as I can. Everything about the city excites me and I couldn't wait to share it with him. We had a hefty schedule of musicals; I worried that Jer might not keep up. I was wrong.

The original cast of "Hamilton" left the show just a few weeks before our tickets, but were still thrilled. Before Wednesday matinees, the cast stood in front of the main doors and said hello to the throngs of fans, and typically sang something, HAM4HAM, they called it. We got there early, in the sea of people and clapped and cheered.

August is a very hot, muggy time to be in the city. Jer had a jacket in hand all day that day which I thought was slightly odd. But everything is so air conditioned, I figured maybe he brought it for me.

The show was magical. I wanted to linger a bit afterward. I wanted to peruse the souvenirs. I wanted to just experience the atmosphere but Jer was so hopped up and energetic. Without any thought at all, he walked up to the souvenir counter, bought himself a t-shirt, a zip-up hoodie for me and we were out of the theater walking toward Times Square before I knew what was happening.

He was eager for me to listen to a song. "Here put these in, listen to this song - help me with the words." I couldn't fathom what the urgency was or why we were trying to listen to a song as afternoon matinees were letting out. Better yet, why we were trying to listen to a song in Times Square on earbuds at all. But he seemed very committed.

We stood in the noise and lights each wearing one of his earbuds, connected with a cord, listening. I recognized it was a song from "Hamilton."

"Eliza I don't have a dollar to my name, an acre of land, a troop to command..." Jer was singing along, but he was getting the words wrong. I looked up to correct him (hey, he said he wanted my help) and he was reading a paper..... "We'll buy a little place in Midvale and we'll figure it out....." It was the song in "Hamilton" where Alexander is asking Eliza's dad for his blessing, a proposal. I didn't know it at the time, but Jer had already picked up a sack of burgers and gone to have a good long talk with my folks about his love for me.

Jeramy had written his own version of the words, unzipped a ring box from that jacket he'd been carrying around and there, in the heart of the Theater District, my favorite place to be, in the greatest city in the world, he was on one knee. I said yes; the crowd went wild.

We took a evening ride on a double-decker bus that rolls through Manhattan - from the sparkle of Times Square, to the grit of the Brooklyn Bridge - a nighttime view of the city that never sleeps. Freshly engaged, our stainless steel water bottles full of something celebratory, Jer announced to the whole top of the bus that we were engaged. The driver played "New York, New York" as the city whizzed by. We laughed about him carrying that jacket around all day, and sang along with Sinatra, stopping only to kiss under the lights from time to time.

Having both been married before, our wedding would be our immediate families only. Small and simple - that's it. We searched for venues which were pricier than we hoped so we thought about an outdoor ceremony. Outdoor events in September can get a little risky in Utah as Mother Nature can take a turn, but we didn't want to wait any longer.

We thought about parks, wondered about having it in someone's yard. I finally had the thought to show Jeramy a tree-lined walking path the Zoo recently installed. It was more of a bridge that stretched out over Emigration Creek, with trees covering anything that looked like the zoo - felt more like a tree house. It was pretty, we wouldn't have to pay and we could likely squeeze it in before the weather turned.

Between the Zoo's daytime and evening events the timing looked tricky but I finally zeroed in on September 24.

I texted him: "How does Sept. 24 sound to become my husband?"

He responded: "It doesn't sound soon enough but I'll take it!"

My mom and I went to the mall in search of a dress. I didn't care if it was white or not, just something affordable that I felt great in. I found a white sheath dress with a lace overlay that just felt right.

I gathered the girls around the computer to look at dresses. We found beautiful orange, sleeveless dresses online that all three girls actually liked.

Jer would create a little bit of a frenzy by deciding the week of our wedding that he wanted to wear a suit after all. I told him nice pants and a shirt would be fine since he didn't own a suit, but he wanted a suit so off we went. We all hopped in Goldie on the Tuesday before our wedding and headed to Mens Warehouse. While charming the workers, he tried on various suits finally settling on a charcoal gray suit and black tie with a purple and white, dotted pattern. He stood looking the mirror beaming - he felt like a groom.

The morning of the wedding, Jer picked up the girls while I got my hair and nails done. I popped into, you guessed it, Costco, to get a cake and flowers and that was it. That was the most stress our wedding day caused. None at all.

Our ceremony was right after the Zoo closed, as the sun was setting; we had the place to ourselves - just us and our immediate families; the people who meant the most to us. The pastor from our church had written lovely vows and my dear friend agreed to come play music on his guitar while I walked down the aisle, which was my sneaky way to get a guitar there without Jeramy suspecting anything.

I wanted to surprise him and had been secretly preparing a song. He loved my singing and it's how I best express myself. I thought of all the amazing love songs in the world - all the songs that would sum up our idyllic love story. But I also sang at my first wedding so I was aware that sometimes the love songs go awry, or maybe I felt sheepish to be doing this again. I needed a song that both captured our love but also captured an awareness that we'd both done this before and here we are, brave enough to try it again.

The song that kept presenting itself to me was "I Hope You're the End of my Story," by Pistol Annies. At the time I liked it because it was a love song with just a little bit of wisdom to it. Maybe it was a non-traditional choice. The me today reads the words and thinks now it feels slightly foreboding. But it's beautiful -

"....I'll keep on turning the pages

Oh, what a story to tell.

You'll sill be my sweetheart when everything ages

You'll be the last book on the shelf.

I hope you're the end of my story,

I hope you're as far as it goes.

I hope you're the last word, I ever utter

And it's never your time to go."

We were married. It was official. We served the cake, and everyone packed up and wandered out of the Zoo, stopping to listen to the lions roar and take a few selfies.

Jeramy and I had our girls that weekend and we wanted it that way. We had what we called a "Familymoon." We took our girls home, did more celebrating, took lots of pictures and the next morning, Jeramy whipped up breakfast. Simple and sweet.

LOVE AND MARRIAGE

You know how we sometimes have inexplicable worries that just nag the back of our brain? Mine was "as soon as we're married it'll all change." I just worried we'd get complacent, that we might not do as many fun things, that we might quit putting forth effort for one another, that it would be different.

I know... I should have known Jer better than that. Nothing changed at all, at least not in that way. What *did* change was that I felt more valuable - my role increasing with his girls, I felt more taken care of and we loved being official. I think there was this collective pride in what we were creating. Even Jer's daughter, a teenager by now, would post #familygoalz on her Instagram posts. Everything just felt right.

They moved into my two bedroom apartment. We put his belongings in storage, got a bunk bed for the kids and did our best to create space even though we were bursting at the seams, we still sort of made it work.

With no kitchen table, we gathered around the kitchen bar, for family meals, Jer and I standing. We didn't have our TV hooked up for the longest time so there weren't any family movie nights. Instead, we sat outside, watching the sun set, watching the girls practice gymnastics, going on walks along the Jordan

River. Jer made cookies whenever we got the craving. He and I muddled our way through figuring out family dinners on our kid weekends.

As we ticked over into the new year, we had a few goals in mind: Get through my upcoming February performance, take a belated honeymoon and find a bigger place to live.

I was booked again at The Grand Theater - the place I performed Patsy so many times before. This was part of their Backstage series which meant an intimate setting, only 100 people or so, a small ensemble and whatever I wanted to sing. I settled on an evening of Broadway songs with my favorite musicians. As you'd imagine, Jer was my most enthusiastic supporter - telling everyone he knew I was performing, even when I preferred he didn't (think cashiers and servers). He sent flowers, he came to dress fittings, he attended all three shows.

I wanted to surprise him with a song. We were newlyweds, a large percentage of the audience had known me for years, and I wanted to share our happiness. I told them the story of meeting this handsome man at Costco, shared that we were now married and sang "Warm All Over," from the Broadway musical, "The Most Happy Fella."

"Warm all over,

Warm all over.

Every time you smile, you get me warm… all over."

I couldn't look at him while I sang. That was a highlight for my audience - many sharing, even years later - how much they loved the story and the song.

Our belated honeymoon would take us back to NYC for another musical whirlwind. This trip came about because of Jer's chattiness with anybody and everybody. He and I sat on the patio of a brew pub in Southern Utah and he struck up a conversation with another couple. They were from New York and were vacationing in the outdoors. They loved Utah. They loved skiing. They loved our mountains and Jer and I happened to live 20 minutes from Big Cottonwood Canyon.

Next thing we knew, a February house swap was in the works. New York was my favorite place and our ski resorts were theirs. We deep-cleaned our house, hooked up our TV (finally) and made sure they had access to our garage.

Their apartment was a dream. Small but tidy, walking distance to Central Park, with a little balcony. We even saw Today show host, Hoda Kotb, in the lobby - ha! (She was very nice, there visiting a friend).

The night we arrived, we walked to the Duane Reade on the corner hoping they'd have wine. While our host couple said we could drink anything they had, we felt a bit sheepish so we ventured out.

We sat on the balcony with our wine. We were most the way through the bottle and just didn't feel that wonderful little buzz we were hoping for after a day of travel. Jer took a closer look at the bottle and discovered we bought a "Wine like product" - we were sitting there drinking freaking fruit juice! We went in and helped ourselves to a bit of their whiskey, promising to find a better bottle the next day.

That February, the weather was sunny, warm even. We rented bikes and biked through Central Park (much hillier than I anticipated). It would also be Jer's introduction to the New York City hot dog. He'd proceed to eat his weight in hot dogs throughout the weekend until his body couldn't take anymore and he spent most of the flight home not feeling super great.

We came home and began looking for a new place to live and Jer busied himself looking for a new job. Wendy's had become unbearable and he was anxious to get out of there. He pursued both those tasks with his usual gusto.

With interviews lined up during the day, we'd go out as a family in the evening and walk through potential rental properties, the girls weighing in on which bedroom they'd like. About the time we found our new place, Jer accepted a new job with Alpha Warranty Services. They do car warranties - believe it or not, his dream job. I chuckled as most people do not dream of selling car warranties but he loved cars and he loved that world - he had been a car salesman in his early years and also owned his own dealership for a time.

Just like the night Jer and I picnicked on the floor of my new apartment before I moved in, he set up a candle light burrito night for the two of us at our new place as well - a three bedroom, two and half bath townhome with an unfinished basement to store all of Jer's 40+ totes of Christmas decor, snowmobile gear, and other mementos he'd been dragging around since high school.

With the girls in their own bedrooms, Jer in his new job and us in our new space, we settled into a routine. Couple-time every other weekend and family-time on the others. Jer did a soft boiled egg extravaganza on Saturdays, the girls helped me plant flowers along our little walkway, and we had rousing family games of Uno, even creating some of our own rules.

We worked on ways to streamline the mundane tasks of running of the household. We downloaded an app that was to serve as a joint grocery shopping list. If I noticed we were out of peanut butter, I could put it on the list then whichever one of us was at the store, could open the app and see an up-to-date list of what needed to be bought. You could also create To Do lists for yourself or spouse in that app - a digital honey-do list of sorts. I began to chuckle as my to-do list filled up with "Be you because you are the greatest! OXOX" "Kiss your husband" then the to-do list ended up just serving as messages. "I love you!" and "I love you more than I ever thought I could love. I'm so grateful for everything you are and everything you do for me and for us!"

Jer and I sat in our double camp chair pretty much any time

the weather allowed - often pushing the boundaries of good weather; wrapped in blankets, wearing hoodies and such. Our townhome living situation meant no private outdoor space, so we sat in the driveway.

Coffee out there in the mornings on weekends, wine out there well, nightly. My feet in his lap, him squeezing my feet and running his hands along my legs.

We'd say hi to the neighbors out on dog walks, even planned a double date with one couple. They joked about us being out there all the time and Jer said "You can call us the boozy twosies!"

When we had the kids, they'd join us out there. We called it driveway time. We'd all just hang out in the driveway and all of our neighbors knew they'd find us there during the summer. Well, spring, summer, and into the fall.

We talked about life, made plans for the future and had great discussions about the gift of this relationship. As Jer called it, we sat and "talked about how awesome we are."

Our driveway time got a bit limited in the summer as the girls decided to be in a musical together. They had never been in a musical before and they were so excited about the idea. We looked up the various community theater productions and their first few auditions didn't go quite as they'd hoped, even with all the effort they put in.

Finally, I caught auditions for "The Music Man," one of my personal favorites, and one that can accommodate a large cast due the number of townsfolk needed. I told Jer I was thinking I ought to do it with them - just to help guide them through auditioning, we could be cast as a package deal, plus I'd be around to sort of keep my eye on things. I just thought that'd be the best way to get the experience we wanted.

I gave up doing summer shows a long time ago as it's not worth it to me to sacrifice my favorite season in a dark, cold theater - even though I love being in a theater. At any rate, we were cast in the show. They would play the various teens and townspeople and I was cast as "Widow Paroo." Naturally we all laughed as I was way too young to play the role of a widow (oh the foreshadowing, am I right?).

So, night after night, we went to rehearsal in a musty old theater, but my heart was sitting in the driveway in the summer-night air. Though I will admit a keen satisfaction the night the director introduced 'cast awards' for the actor who really hit it out of the park that night - Imagine my delight when I won the first candy bar!

We'd come home after rehearsal to Jer waiting for us in the driveway. We'd tell him all about rehearsal and what went on. When the girls went in to shower, I'd take a few sips of his drink and tell him how much I was missing him.

They thrived that summer - they danced, they sang, they learned blocking, they participated in backstage shenanigans, they fussed with their costumes, they made friends, they gained confidence. And I got to witness it all.

Naturally, Jer was at every single performance. He sent flowers and cards with candy. He cheered, he bought concessions, he brought friends. During "76 trombones" our blocking had the cast marching out into the amphitheater and around the audience. Jer tried to catch our eye every night, maybe to make us laugh. When we got toward the back of the theater one night, Jer jumped in and snapped some selfies. We all laughed that night about how confused our characters were at this strange fellow and this strange device in his hand we'd never seen before.

I wrapped up another engagement of Patsy in early September (yes Jer took all sorts of posters to hang up at work) then we were off to an all-inclusive resort in Cancun for our anniversary trip. We'd had such a busy summer and the thought of sitting around gazing at an ocean, drinking cocktails and holding hands sounded just perfect.

A couple of weeks before, we sat on my parents patio telling the fam about our trip. My sis in the travel industry noted 'you might want to make sure that resort is all-inclusive - I don't think it is.' Jer's eyes bulged out of his head at the notion that we could get there, eat and drink with gusto then be zinged with a bill at the end. He immediately started making calls. With his phone on speaker, he explained his mistake to the various phone people all while sitting on the patio chatting with my family.

Crisis averted (thanks sis), and we were off. Everything about that trip was perfection. From the moment we got off that plane and felt that tropical air, we were in our own paradise. Jer spoke Spanish everywhere we went making every server, karaoke host, bartender and housekeeper our best friends. I don't know what he said, but every one of them giggled and laughed and posed for selfies with him.

We enjoyed poolside chips and guac (lots of it), he tried all the fruity cocktails he could find, I preferred my tried and true Tanqueray and tonic. We went to some shows, we loved our fancy dinners. It was so carefree - we never left the resort.

We wandered through the gift shops at one point, after I lingered a bit at the window of a jewelry store. They had everything from gems and stones to simpler silver and gold bands. My eye caught a ring with a large, oval, dark green stone. The worker, unsure of the stone, let me try it on and I loved it. It was roughly $100 American dollars and I hemmed and hawed cause I didn't really need a souvenir that was quite that much money and I just wasn't sure. I decided I'd think about it and we left the store empty handed.

The next day Jer and I got a bottle of wine and wandered down to the seaside cabanas - no one was around. Just us and that beautiful, endless sea. Our waitress wandered over from time to time (yes, more guac please) and we sat and chatted and smooched and laughed and touched and drank and kissed some more. There was a potential storm on the horizon which cast dramatic lighting across the ocean, the blues fading into dark greens until it met the brooding sky.

I watched Jer as he walked back to me, after getting wet, the ocean water clinging to his strong frame. He sat down, kissed me and smiled. His eyes were the exact color of the green in the ocean behind him. The exact color of that ring. I decided I needed that ring to remind me of this moment, of this day, of this precious time together, of his eyes.

That night Jer charmed everyone with a rousing version of "Friends in Low Places" at the resort's karaoke night. He ended up convincing another guy into a duet and they sang their hearts out. We all sang along but not before I was put on the spot to warble my way through "My Heart Will Go On." Jer told everyone that I was a singer and that was the hostesses favorite song. Good lord. Look, there is singing and then there is Celine Dion. I don't come anywhere near her pipes - enormously powerful. But there I was, luckily most had been drinking, myself included. There came those big notes and I was determined to hit vaguely in the vicinity and Jer whooped and hollered and so did everyone else. (I still wonder if my vocal cords have forgiven me for that night).

With the green stone ring on my hand, and a new red sun hat in the other, it was time to leave our paradise, vowing that would be our annual anniversary tradition - sun, guac, drinks, relaxation and each other.

We slipped into autumn, Jer dressing up as a gangster for the office Halloween party, knocking himself out fixing a taco soup when Victoria's grandparents came for visit and of course making his butternut squash cobbler for Thanksgiving.

Jer's job was progressing just as he'd hoped. He was traveling a bit, making great friends of his agents in the field and with the tuition reimbursement, he decided he ought to sign on and get his MBA.

He participated in every contest, game, you-name-it that Alpha came up with including the August fitness challenge. Jer pulled out his old bike and got it tuned up. He biked to and from work every day for a month putting two inches on his thighs and an inch on each calf - he was freaky that way, able to bulk up with minimal effort. Much to the dismay of well, every man he knew.

I'd heard so many stories about his coworkers, I was excited to meet them all at the Alpha Christmas party. The event was in downtown Salt Lake City at the Grand America, Salt Lake's only AAA Five Diamond Hotel. Jer decided we ought to make a night of it and get a room as well. We planned to get there early, enjoy the pool and spa then head to the fancy dinner.

We climbed out of the hot tub and put on our robes. Jer grabbed a handful of pretzels out of the dish at the reception desk, handing a few to me as well. With wet hair and a wad of clothing under our arms, we made our way to the elevator. The last thing I said to Jer was "Listen, I don't want to run into any of your coworkers looking like this."

I could see it happening in slow motion. A cute couple down the hallway, walking toward the elevator, Jer's face changing in acknowledgement and me starting to say 'noooooooooo!' But before I could, Jer's arm was outstretched in a big wave as the couple walked closer. Yes I turned to run back into the spa. I tried hiding. It was too late.

"Hi!" the two men greeted one another.

"This is my lovely wife, Erica!" There I stood with a mouthful of pretzels, wet hair, no makeup, holding a crumpled up ball of clothing. "And this is my boss Brian."

Brian introduced his adorable wife and the elevator doors opened. So, we all got in and tried to make small talk, Jer and I standing there wet, in our robes. At least we had something to laugh about at the fancy dinner later that night.

I don't entirely remember how it transpired. But sometime after the Alpha party and before Christmas, Jer sent Victoria and me to New York City. We found a deal and I mentioned it'd be a dream to share my favorite city with her. He insisted. "You don't know if we'll be able to make it happen again and this year we can. Go."

For a long weekend, it was just my kid and me - seeing Broadway shows, seeing The Rockettes, and trekking down to see Hamilton's resting spot at Trinity Church - twice (they were closed the first time). It was a dream. It was a chance to share one of my great loves with her and it was a chance to get to know her better - we still chuckle about our various jokes from that trip.

That December we also got a bit of good news - Our love story was selected to be featured in the Costco CONNECT magazine! I'd submitted our love story *months* prior after reading about it in their monthly magazine. The charge? Tell us your Costco love story. The post said something like, "Did you meet at Costco? Get engaged at Costco? Did Costco play a pivotal role in your love story? We want to hear about it!"

We got all geeked up as we knew that very few could top our Costco love story - it served as a beautiful backdrop to our story since day one. I was determined to submit. I knew we'd get selected, if only I could write our submission well enough to catch their eyes.

I worked on it and submitted in August some time. Getting that December notice that we were going to be featured had us all laughing.

They would edit what I submitted but they wanted to print our photo along with the story in the February / Valentine's edition.

Here's what they ran:

We met at Costco.

Our first encounter after we met, he brought me Costco churros.

He sent me on a scavenger hunt to Costco.

We went on a date in the Costco parking lot to celebrate our one-year dating anniversary.

He proposed with a ring from Costco.

We cut a Costco cake at our wedding.

We used Costco flowers.

And our first Christmas cards as a new family were, of course, from Costco.

We're about to celebrate our one-year anniversary and could not be happier. Your long aisles and breadth of variety have left us with a standing date (samples!), new eyeglasses, a photo book of our proposal trip to New York, new shirts as Jeramy started a new career and many sweet memories.

Kirkland Signature means quality and value, and that's exactly what I got in my Kirkland Signature-brand husband: He's a dream

Thank you Costco!

Christmas was looming and we had the girls that year. When my sis mentioned she was going to do fondue with her family, Jer and I thought that sounded fun. Before I could refill my glass, he'd ordered us a fondue pot off of Amazon.

We almost botched the fondue event, saved once again by my sis who told us there was more to fondue than melting a block of cheddar (thanks sis). We ate our fondue, decorated gingerbread houses, and wore matching sweatsuits.

Jer had participated in Movember - the annual event where men don't shave their faces during November to raise awareness for men's health issues. November turned into December for Jer and the girls hated it. They did not like him with a beard and told him so - often.

That night, after they'd gone to bed, Jer shaved his face clean for a Christmas morning surprise. It took them a while to realize it, then we all howled and cheered, they leapt in his arms and rubbed his smooth face.

The last weekend of the year, it was just us. Jer had been keeping his eye on end-of-year new car close-outs. Goldie was on her last leg and it was time to upgrade.

We'd been test driving various makes and models for comparison, I had no idea what kind of car I wanted. Jer was relentless, texting various car salesmen ensuring we got the best deal. We drove everything from minivans to massive SUVs.

We started to narrow in on the Jeep Grand Cherokees. I liked a deep red, the color of a nice Cabernet, and I liked the chrome finish. Many times I told Jer it didn't have to be THAT exactly but he couldn't be swayed.

Through all his finagling, we finally got word that the dealership had one. A beautiful red Jeep Grand Cherokee with chrome finish and tan leather interior, 4WD, heated seats AND a heated steering wheel. It was a dream and my sweetheart stopped at nothing to make sure it was mine.

We drove home - I had a huge smile and so much gratitude. Jer handled everything and when I thanked him for his efforts he said "I just remember you saying Goldie didn't fit the sophisticated image you wanted to project. And I thought to myself then - I'm going to get this woman into the car of her dreams some day."

And he did.

I'M GOIN' TO NASHVILLE

Matty and I ate lunch on a patio one beautiful fall afternoon. He was on one of his frequent trips back to SLC. We try to meet for lunch, dinner or drinks every time he visits. We caught up on my new married life, the girls, how great Jer and I were doing and as he caught me up on life in L.A., he said he was going to Nashville for work. I perked right up and said 'I want to meet you there' he enthusiastically agreed that I should.

I'm sure you, like me, can't figure out why I hadn't already been there. It's not in the far reaches of the earth, it's filled with everything I love - music, history, Patsy, The Grand Ol' Opry, everything -my dream come true. I was ecstatic and quite eager. Matty and I hadn't traveled together for a while and since Jer and I were without the girls that weekend, I was pretty sure we could arrange it so he could also join for part of it. So we started planning.

Matty would be in Nashville for the week and could easily stay through the weekend. I would fly in on Wednesday, stay in his room, get some solo time in the city while he wrapped up two days of work but we'd have the evenings to pal around like our good ol' days.

Jeramy was going to work in Atlanta that week then rent a car on Friday morning, drive the four hours to Nashville and be there by lunchtime. We were all going to enjoy a weekend of live music, the Opry, the Patsy Museum, with great food and drinks. I was so excited to finally experience Nashville but more excited that Matty and Jer would have the chance to get to know one another better. It would be a dream.

And it was... for a day.

ONE PERFECT DAY

I have a selfie with the wall of gold records and one with a Patsy Cline plaque. A random photo of a band I sat listening to. One from my seat showing the view at the Ryman. Those were the last photos I took. I remember the day exquisitely for its surreal perfection prior to its tragic turn.

When we lose someone unexpectedly, our brains sear memories into the landscape - like a controlled burn almost - of life before / life after. The great divide. Making those last moments of your 'old life' when you were happily existing so vividly crisp; almost tangible.

I remember, as I strolled around alone, wishing people could see me with my sweetheart; that they'd see what happiness looks like.

I remember forgetting to tip the Uber driver.

I remember watching people eat biscuits.

I arrived in Nashville on Wednesday; I was geeked up the second I got off the plane - ads for the Country Music Hall of Fame, ads for the Songwriters Hall of Fame, billboards for the Patsy museum. The place is crawling with music, country music, and I just couldn't wait to get out into the city.

I took an Uber to the hotel and Matty and I spent the evening roaming around, we popped into a few bars, wandered around the Ryman, which seems plopped strangely in the middle of everything. He and I took a hotel room selfie when we realized we'd dressed almost identically in olive green shirts and black pants. I swapped a few texts with Jer who was still in Atlanta, but we didn't talk.

Thursday was one of the most perfectly magical days of my life. Other than the steady rain, I couldn't have designed a better day for myself which now seems sort of ominous. Matty worked that day so I had the day all to myself. A day of nothing but nerding out alone about country music, songwriters, Patsy, live music just everything that I'm nerdier about than most. I borrowed an umbrella from the hotel, stepped outside, took a deep breath and just felt excited to be standing on a brink of a day full of so much potential.

I found a breakfast spot specializing in southern biscuits. The place was packed but they had a table for one open. I made a mental note that this was a great little walkable breakfast spot when Jer and Matty were with me.

After biscuits (and likely bacon), I walked toward the heart of Nashville and spent the first half of the day in the Country Music Hall of Fame and Museum. I got to just quietly roam and read every little sign that interested me. They had temporary exhibits of Shania Twain's costumes; a Loretta Lynn tribute (she was a great friend of Patsy Cline's) and mementos from country power-couple Tim McGraw and Faith Hill.

I got to see gold records, lyrics scratched out on napkins and various instruments on which some amazing songs were recorded. I was there alone and while there are parts I would have loved to share with someone, I was grateful to just go at my own pace and explore. Do you know what a gift that is? To have unlimited time doing something you love without having to gauge anyone else's interest?

At the end of the museum portion, you enter the rotunda - the actual hall of fame featuring the plaques of all the honorees. I felt a strange, not quite eerie, but a profound something being in that space. It was almost.. Hmm.. scary is not quite the right word... humbling or I don't know, just the magnitude. I know others wander through, take a few quick glances and wander out. But not me. I spent a fair amount of time in there, looking at the plaques, finding Patsy's, just feeling the reverence. I felt small.

The second I stepped out of the rotunda, I heard music. There was a choir set up in the lobby singing a cappella - it was beautiful. The choir geek in me teared up - actually that happened throughout the day at numerous points. I couldn't figure out if they had just begun at that moment, or if I was so lost in my reverie in the rotunda that I didn't hear them.

On my way out of the museum, I stopped by the box office for the CMA Theater to look at the performance schedule, wondering if there would be a concert we'd all enjoy. Country star Travis Tritt was performing for two nights doing his acoustic set. The shows were sold out, but I put our names on the waiting list, crossing my fingers that something would open up.

I wandered in the drizzle toward the Ryman Auditorium - the original home of the Grand Ol' Opry. Everyone has performed there - from Elvis to Johnny Cash to Patsy Cline to Paul Simon, B.B. King; comedians, musicians, a wide array of artists. I just wanted to sit with it, if that makes sense. Look at it's beautiful red brick facade, imagine people lined up to get in. I just wanted to go there and be in its presence. I'm sure it's the same for baseball fans and Fenway Park or art lovers at The Met - you just want to sit in its presence; see what you can feel.

Naturally I already researched who or what might be performing at the Ryman while we were there. March 1 was the season kick-off to the Opry Country Classics series. The evening was hosted by Larry Gatlin of the Gatlin brothers, that's all I knew. But I also knew I simply had to see a show in there. I didn't know if I should, I could hang out with Matty that night; would Jer want to see a show; was there anything good playing tomorrow night? I walked up to the box office and wouldn't you know it, the night would be a tribute to Johnny Cash. Well, Johnny and June Carter Cash, their love story AND, Mandy Barnett, who played the role of Patsy in the original production of "Always... Patsy Cline," was also performing. I assumed it was meant to be. Matty said I should just go ahead and go - he had a work dinner and would meet me later. I texted Jer who was delighted I'd be seeing a show at the Ryman. I bought the ticket for that night's show and headed back out to explore.

The main drag through Nashville is Broadway - one bar after another which means, it's nothing but live music, upon live music, upon live music, at seemingly all times of the day. The music trickles out onto the sidewalk through open windows and doors; people gather, listen a second and either go in or move to the next. Many of the bars are covered in history too - mementos, trinkets, so-and-so played here. I found a spot, grabbed a beer and a snack while listening to the band that drew me in.

I went to the Patsy museum next. This was a special experience for me. It's a small museum and I had all the time in the world to spend as much time as I wanted. Naturally I was waiting for something magical to happen, something other-worldly; some sign from Patsy. It didn't. But that didn't dampen my enjoyment at all. I got to see a few photos I'd never seen before and just feel her essence a bit.

Side note, as we were planning this trip, sweet Jer reached out to the guy who runs the Patsy Cline museum and asked if there was anything special they could do for me. I think he actually boldly asked if I'd be able to meet Jennifer, Patsy's daughter - ha! He was still exchanging messages with the guy while I was there but hadn't quite finalized anything.

I strolled along Broadway listening to the various music offerings, and picked out a bar with the right mood, a good people-watching crowd and decent menu to kill a bit of time before my show at the Ryman.

I pined for Jer all day long. I liked enjoying the city alone but I simply could not wait for him to be there, to be one of those couples like the ones I was watching. I sat off to the side, ordered my food and thought 'all of you wait until my man is here - you'll see.' At 5:44 p.m. I texted him two GIFs - an animated drawing of a couple hugging, the woman's fingers running up into her man's hair and a big fat cat slumped over with 'I miss you.' I texted him 'I sure miss you.' He responded 'Oh I sure miss you too babe, have a good time.' That would be our last communication. The last thing I sent was a big fat cat GIF (yes, you can probably figure out how I feel about that).

There have been many times since Jer's passing that I've remembered this moment. This moment in the bar and how deeply I yearned to have him there. How content I was in the moment - music, food, drinks - but how much I missed him; how much fun we'd be having if he were with me; how much better everything was when he was around. It's strange to think I was getting some type of foreshadowing of my new life right in that moment in a Nashville bar.

The Ryman Auditorium. The Mother Church of Country Music.

Historians will tell you this isn't just a concert hall - it's hallowed ground. The building was built in the late 1800s to serve as an evangelical place of worship and was turned into a concert hall in the 1920s. Considered the 'Carnegie of the South,' The Ryman remains a much sought-after place for performers of all genres. The wrap-around church pews and acoustics - designed to enhance the booming voices of evangelists - make it a premiere venue to this day.

I know I've said it before but it bears repeating - This was a really big deal for me. This building holds the spirits of an extraordinary amount of performers, Patsy included. Its history is legendary and I was about to see a show there.

The Ryman's website says it best: *The Ryman was originally built for people to experience something transformative together.* Transformative is the best word for what I experienced that night.

I had a single seat on the first row of the balcony, right in the center. The 'best seat in the house,' according to the usher. I sat between two men on either side who were there with their wives. I had a lone single seat, and a straight-shot view to center stage.

The Opry Country Classics series is broadcast on WSM radio. The evening began with the announcer motioning for all of us to begin clapping for background noise while he announced the sponsors and such. The band kicked in, the Gatlin Brothers sang "All the Gold in California," and "Houston." Again, having grown up with my folks listening to country, I knew these songs. The brothers bantered with each other, Mandy Barnett came out and sang a couple of songs accompanying herself on the ukulele.

That's when the evening took an interesting turn, the Gatlins returned to the stage and began their tribute to Johnny Cash and June Carter Cash - easily the most iconic love story in country music. Throughout the evening the brothers shared stories about how in love Johnny and June were. I smiled thinking about the love story I was living with Jer and how all those sweet stories and lyrics could apply to us. The brothers would tell a story, gesture to heaven toward Johnny and June and sing.

This was March 1, 2018, not long after the passing of preacher Billy Graham. The Gatlin Brothers got their start singing gospel and they're known for their tight, three-part harmonies on these classics. At one point they came out to honor Graham and had audience members shout out which gospel song they wanted to hear. While I don't remember any specific songs, I do remember they nailed each and every one. They pointed up to the sky, often. I teared up numerous times at the beauty of the music and how genuinely they treated the material. All night long, love stories, goosebumps, gospel music, tears - it was magical, I was transfixed.

I walked out of the Ryman feeling like I'd had a religious experience. My musical soul had been filled to the brim, the gospel music moved me, the gratitude from the performers for the gift of music echoed my own thoughts from the evening. I couldn't have been happier or more content. I stepped out onto the noisy streets, turned and gave one last look at the Ryman before heading to meet Matty. I was truly filled.

LONGEST, DARKEST NIGHT

I met Matty in Tootsie's Lounge for an end-of-day, post-show drink and more live music. Tootsie's is a Nashville institution. I knew of Tootsie's through my years of Patsy research. The honky-tonk is across the alley from the Ryman. Performers and songwriters would gather there to tell jokes, swap song lyrics. Patsy, Willie Nelson, Kris Kristofferson - everyone went to Tootsie's. The owner at the time was nice to up-and-coming songwriters and Tootsie's plays backdrop to some of the greatest music we love today. The walls almost vibrate with history.

The place was packed - elbow to elbow, sitting on top of one another, brushing body to body to get up to the bar. We were lucky to find a stool to share. I sat, took a sip of beer and took a deep breath.

I checked my phone and had a missed call from Jer's sister, Dawn, in Atlanta. I kind of croaked - we had just gotten settled, I'd have to work my way outside of the bar to hear or be heard and I really wanted to just sit here with Matty and enjoy the music. For a split second I thought about finishing the beer then calling her back, but it was odd she called me so I thought better of waiting.

I told Matty I had to make a call and I'd be right back. I worked my way out of the sandwiched-in spot, past the bar, past the bandstand, out onto the street and called Dawn.

I couldn't hear her. The music from all the bars was chaos, the energy of Broadway was picking up, people were out in force.

"Dawn hold on I can't hear you, let me step in here." There was a gift shop next door to Tootsie's full of touristy kitsch - ash trays, key chains, coffee mugs, hoodies etc. I stepped inside, out of the noise, and stood leaning on a round rack of shirts, next to the wall of t-shirt cubicles.

"Okay now I can hear you," I said.

"Erica, I'm so sorry but Jeramy's passed away," Dawn managed to eke out.

My world stopped while at the same time started spinning.

"What?!"

"Jeramy's passed away."

I'm sure she said it again. My memory of this moment starts to get quite hazy. I know I squatted down. I know that didn't make me feel better so I stood back up. I don't remember much of our short conversation. She must have told me they think it was blood clots because I think I remember knowing that.

The call was brief, I don't know how it ended - how do you wrap up a call like that? Did we make a plan? I stood there in the fluorescent lighting, wondering if I'd puke or if I should tell the worker or something.

I do remember knowing that while everything felt strangely the same, I knew I was existing in a world that was profoundly different from the one I was in not even three minutes ago. The desire to pull a Superman and start spinning the world backward was overwhelming. Jer was still SO close in that moment I knew if I acted quickly, that I could still reach him somehow.

I thought about that brand new beer I'd only taken one sip out of. If only I finished it - I would still be there in that world - a world with Jer in it; I could've made it last longer.

I don't remember crying. I was more in a state of utter shock and disbelief. I walked toward the door, the clerk chirped "Thanks for coming in!" I stepped onto the street and there was Matty wondering where I'd gone and if everything was okay.

I blurted out "Jeramy died."

"WHAT?!"

"They think he had blood clots."

There we stood in the middle of Nashville's Broadway, with all its crazy, country fun happening around us. And there I stood looking in the face of one of my most-trusted souls, Matty Wall, who I'd now trust to navigate me through a crowded Broadway and back to the hotel.

He pulled out his phone, ordered an Uber and we began heading to the meeting spot. I was in a stunned stupor, still not crying, walking around in a confused daze. I took one step off a curb and some drunk women started shouting at me "HA! YOU MIGHT WANT TO GET OUT OF THE ROAD!!!!" laughing with her friends at how bold she was. I turned and locked eyes with her, conjuring up all the things I could say and Matty touched my arm and said "No, no." I turned back and our driver pulled up.

He was making small talk which luckily Matty handled. I just sat there; I said nothing. Matty guided me back to our hotel room. I remember saying "oh what do I do? What do I do?"

I called my mom; she just tucked Victoria in bed. I remember thinking how she would want to go back to tucking in Victoria and back to a world where Jer existed, not be in this new one.

While I don't remember much about our conversation, I do remember wailing "Who's going to marry me now?!" as though getting myself remarried was my first concern.

We say stupid things in that moment. What I was trying to communicate was: 'No one will love me as fully and as selflessly as Jeramy did. No one will ever come close to rising to the bar that Jer set. It took me a while; I finally found him. I've just lost the MOST extraordinary husband a person could have. Am I to be alone for the rest of my life?'

My mom, reeling in her own shock sweetly said "Well, we won't worry about that right now, sis."

According to Psychology Today, the hallmark symptom of shock is a surge of adrenaline. That surge may make you feel like you're going to throw up or have diarrhea, which happened in that moment and would be something I'd experience over and over for the next couple of weeks. I apologized to Matty but also couldn't bring myself to care much beyond that.

Dawn was in Atlanta, Jeramy was too, at least his body was. I decided I needed to rent a car and get to Atlanta; I knew I couldn't wait for a next day flight. Matty must have arranged the Uber for us as I threw all my belongings in the suitcase. The Nashville airport was the only car rental place still open at this hour. I said my goodbyes to Matty, he had work to finish and made me promise I'd be okay.

I got in the car, hooked up my phone and set out on my trek to Atlanta; telling my mom it's all I knew to do and I'd text her when I arrived. Nashville loomed behind me in the rearview mirror and I couldn't get out of there fast enough.

Dawn lived just outside Atlanta in Flowery Branch, GA, making the drive just over four hours long; including the time zone difference, I'd arrive around 4 a.m. According to Google Maps, it's mostly a straight shot on I-24, until it turns into I-75. Also according to Google Maps, the route looks like it passes through quite a few towns - Manchester, Dalton, Calhoun and a few major ones too - Chattanooga and Murfreesboro, that one I've never heard of but it's bold on the map so it must be sizable.

That's notable to me as I remember absolutely none of it. I don't remember seeing one city or town. I don't remember city lights. Just blackness. Utter nighttime, dark and blackness. That's why I looked it up on the map as I wrote this. I was curious if I was driving through nothingness, as I remember, or if there was actual civilization along that major freeway.

I set out in darkness and my whole drive would be in darkness. I remember being so grateful for navigation help as I never could have managed map-reading. I drove in the quiet the whole time asking myself 'is this real?! This is the stuff you hear about happening to other people.'

I glanced at the clock and caught 11:33 - a magic number for us. 11s and 33s have special meaning in the angel and spirit world. My new-agey girlfriend was keen on numerology and Jer and I had fun with it so we paid attention when we saw those. Jer's favorite number was 33 - his preference had more to do with NASCAR but my girlfriend always gushed about the significance of 33 as well. This moment was my first sampling of all those scenes you see in movies where someone receives a message from elsewhere. I caught the 11:33 and gasped - is this my new life now? Looking for clues? Looking for signs? Jer is that you? Are you with me on this drive? (I'm now 100% convinced he was).

Dawn called. "Erica, do you want to donate Jeramy's tissue? If you do, time is important and they need to get working. They have to take his body in now - they can't wait for you to get here." I knew without hesitation that Jer would want to donate anything and everything they could possibly take. I winced because I thought I would get to see him and also because once they start taking his body parts he cannot come back to life.

Another phone call from the organ and tissue donation people. What a job - can you imagine? Time is crucial in these matters so they're calling someone in their most absurd, unbearable moment to get the necessary permission and information.

They're sorry for my loss, they're grateful for the donation. For the next 30 minutes or so they asked all sorts of questions about my sweetheart - How old was he; did he smoke; did he drink; did he have tattoos - how many, how long ago; had he had sex with a man; did he do drugs; had he had a transfusion, so on and so forth.

"Mr. Evans will be able to donate a lot of tissue including eyes or corneas, veins, valves...." More silence and darkness. They're going to take his eyes. They're going to take those beautiful dark green eyes. Huh. His eyes.

Dawn called. 'Erica, they have to take him now. I'm so sorry. The only thing I can think to do is FaceTime you so you can see him one last time.' At that moment, a truck stop appeared out of the darkness and I was able to pull over. I sat under the fluorescent lights of the truck stop otherwise surrounded by darkness. Dawn switched to video and flipped the camera around. There was my Jeramy, my handsome, my hunky. There he was looking like himself and also not a bit like himself. He was in one of those stupid hospital gowns, he had a breathing apparatus strapped to his face. He just laid there. I don't remember crying. I remember feeling exceptionally cold. I remember wanting to touch him but couldn't because I was sitting who knows where at a magical truck stop that appeared out of nowhere. I remember thinking I should be crying. I remember thinking 'Dawn is watching and she's not going to believe that I'm sad - I should be crying and wailing.' I just looked at him; looked and got back on the road.

I've come to learn more about the brain and how it handles and processes shock and trauma. While I was bizarrely worried that I didn't perform well enough for Dawn to believe I was sad, my brain was working hard to keep me alive; to protect me; to manage all the functions it could possibly handle so I didn't have to think. My brain was doing exactly what it was designed to do - miraculously keeping its vessel alive.

More darkness, a few tail lights and then a larger than life, bright yellow billboard for Zaxby's. I caught my breath. Zaxby's was an ongoing, long-running joke in our house for the lighthearted, flamboyant way Jer would pronounce it. We always joked about Zaxby's just to get him to perform a little bit. In a sea of darkness, there it was, all lit up like a stadium - must've had twenty spotlights on it, and the yellowest thing I've ever seen - Jer's favorite color. Again I asked him if that was him; if he was here with me.

Those are the only things I saw on that long drive - an 11:33, a magical truck stop and the Zaxby's billboard.

Dawn's neighborhood was still very much asleep as I pulled onto her street and up her very long driveway. She met me outside, nodded it was true, gave me a hug and I cried.

10:20 P.M.

Jeramy died unceremoniously, mostly all alone, lying in an emergency room in Atlanta. At least that's what I pieced together.

You see, I wasn't there. His sister wasn't there. The coworker he was working with in Atlanta, wasn't there. His death was called at 10:20 p.m.

Jer drove himself to the hospital after passing out in the shower a couple of times that night — that was after an urgent care sent him home with prescriptions for three different inhalers and one for nausea.

That was it.

I write this over two and a half years later and still shake my head in disbelief. It's utterly absurd that such a big, strappin' hunk of a man, healthy as an ox, (he didn't even have any cavities) so vibrant and full of life, is gone. That he struggled to breathe. That no one was immediately alarmed. That he drove himself to the hospital that night.

As an aside, and so I feel like I'm doing my civic duty: If you can't breathe, you should be alarmed. For a time after Jeramy's death I would tell people 'turns out not being able to breathe is actually a really big deal,' which I know sounds stupid.

But he had doctors tell him everything looked normal. He was told he just had asthma. Blood clots kill 100,000 - 300,000 people a year in the United States, which according to stoptheclot.org, is more than the number of people who die from AIDS, breast cancer and car crashes - **combined.** Can you believe that? One person dies every six minutes from a blood clot. Get this: As many as 900,000 people could be affected by clots and for one out of four of those people, sudden death is the first symptom. Yet we rarely hear about it and it is often misdiagnosed. This is purely anecdotal, but after Jeramy's passing a family doctor (father of a friend) told me he has a post-it note on his computer at work with P.E. written on it to remind him to check for a pulmonary embolism.

I first heard a security guard found him slumped in the car in the parking lot. I envisioned that security guard watching a car pull in erratically, making him notice the driver. I pictured Jer in the driver's seat, unable to get out of the car, alone and scared. I wondered if he called out for me.

The medical examiner's report would tell a different tale - Jeramy made it into the emergency room. He was apparently able to choke out "trouble breathing" and maybe rattle off a few other symptoms before he collapsed. At one point, they even brought him back for a minute and then he was gone again. Those blessed ER doctors worked on my sweetheart for 45 minutes trying to make those big, wonderful lungs of his fill with air. They didn't. They never would again. His strong, beautiful body that I loved, that had protected me, made love to me, danced with me, massaged me, just stopped working.

By the time his sister arrived at the hospital, she and the sweet friend who drove the 50 minute journey, were taken to a back room where a doctor delivered the unthinkable news.

She didn't make it in time. And I.....

Well.... I....

I was sitting in the Ryman, wrapping up a perfect day.

FLOWERY BRANCH

Each story you hear of unexpected, tragic loss has its own set of circumstances. Some people talk about how their home filled up with people bringing noise and food they didn't eat; others might have a sterile hospital scene. Mine was a solo drive through the night to the home of Jeramy's sister, whom I did not know, to stay at a place I'd never been. What a crushing and intimate moment to share with a stranger.

But Dawn went from stranger to lifeline instantly. In fact, in all this time I still haven't found words to adequately describe or fully explain what her role and presence meant to me in those moments. Dawn offered the most profoundly humbling service I've ever witnessed.

A little background on Dawn - She's the eldest of Jeramy's siblings; there are six of them (Jer's number two). She moved out of Utah maybe 30 years ago and is mom to three amazing men, and another on the verge of becoming one. Her husband was out of town that weekend and her youngest, sensing the heavy weight in the home, mostly stayed at a friend's. It was just us two ladies.

Dawn was comfort and serenity; guidance and wisdom. She was a constant shoulder to cry on, one to commiserate with and was an extraordinarily brave steward through some of life's most intense moments. My family, my support system, was over 1,800 miles away, but Dawn was there. Dawn stepped in when my mom could not.

I arrived in those dark, early hours of the day you hope to never see. It was Friday morning and we didn't fly out of Atlanta until Tuesday afternoon. For almost five full days it was Dawn and me getting to know one another while navigating sorrow, grief and logistics.

Dawn didn't say 'he's okay, he gasped back to life' like I knew she would. She just nodded yes and hugged me and I finally broke down - the way I wanted to in that truck stop parking lot when I thought she was watching for my reaction. I called my mom to let her know I'd made it and croaked out, "Mom….. it's true. He's gone."

It was early Friday morning, still dark outside, I stood there crying with a woman I'd only met once before. It was roughly 6 a.m. before I called the girls on FaceTime. It's such a helpless moment delivering news like that. I was calling to upend their world and wasn't there to do anything to help them.

I crawled into the guest bed and I don't remember getting out of bed the rest of the day except for each surge of adrenaline that sent me to the bathroom. I'd come back and just sit in that bed. I sat there staring out the window, crying, staring.

Dawn handled a few more phone calls - to Jer's boss and his coworker in Atlanta. I just sat and stared. I remember one conversation with my sister telling her I'd have to pick out a cemetery for my husband and the grief burst out of my throat in guttural wails, a terrible sound almost inexplicable; unrecognizable. Dawn rushed to my side and hugged me, just sat there holding me for some time. She later brought me one of Jer's shirts; I recognized it as one he packed for the trip. I took a big, large inhale and slipped it on and went back to staring.

"I need paper and a pen," I said. Even in that moment, I knew I was experiencing something that would need processing and that's the way my brain processes. I also knew I wouldn't remember much of what was about to happen - that it would be a fog. I understood that I would want some proof, something tangible, something real. Dawn came right back with a beautiful, unused journal that had the serenity prayer printed on the cover *"God grant me the serenity to accept the things I cannot change, the courage to change the things I can and the wisdom to know the difference."*

As night approached an eerie sense of something crept in - not fear, per se, just darkness. Impending darkness. Fear of the long slog of lying in the night, wide awake, mind racing, few distractions. Wanting to sleep also felt like something trivial - like I should be focused on the sorrow of my life rather than sweet slumber. I didn't want to be alone but I also wanted to be alone. Exhaustion filled every cell - having not slept the night before during the drive, the mental fatigue and emotional burden - I wanted to sleep but was inexplicably afraid to do so and was afraid of waking back up in this world.

Dawn said goodnight, gave me some over-the-counter sleep aid and said she'd be right outside on the sofa if I needed anything. The room looked small and shadowy as I laid there waiting for the sleep stuff to kick in. Would it? Could my body be tricked? Could my mind? I drifted for a few hours.

I noticed the shadows shifting in the room as the morning sun began its journey. Dawn came in with some Starbucks and set it on the bedside table. What a welcome gesture; I took that first and best sip and sat there. As a practicing Mormon, Dawn does not drink coffee or tea, but each morning she brought me Starbucks and at lunchtime she brought me iced tea - Two of my simple comforts in life.

She sat beside me, gently rubbed my leg a bit and talked about her dad writing an obituary, something about a funeral, mentioned a cemetery, funeral home and a few other things. I sipped my coffee and stared.

From the bed I could look out the window to the backyard, a lovely tree-lined expanse bordering the community golf course. If I looked straight ahead, I was looking up the hallway toward the fireplace in the living room of a mysterious house I'd never seen, other than the bathroom right outside my bedroom.

Saturday, just before lunchtime, I clutched the journal and the box of tissues Dawn gave me and wandered out into the great room area. The kitchen was tidy, there was Jer's suitcase. I think I surprised Dawn by being out of bed, she was making calls to Delta for our trip home with Jer's body. Bless her for that as something so complex was well beyond my scope. Most of what Dawn did was beyond my scope. It would be weeks before I realized she did all that while also grieving the loss of her brother.

Standing toward the front of the house, I could see the sun was shining in Flowery Branch, Georgia, and I needed to feel it. Dawn dug out a camp chair and with my journal and tissues - which both became my security blankets - I sat outside on the front walkway and felt the sun on my face. Dawn's home sat up on a hill so the road and passersby were far away and there was no threat of having to interact with anyone - a blessing for me.

It was still quite cold back home and I was desperate for some warmth. This sun was a gift. I just sat there, all day - stuffing used tissues into the chair's cup holders and writing when something needed to be put on paper. Otherwise I sat there, slumped in my chair listening to birds, wondering if they carried secret messages from Jer. I wrote about what was happening. I wrote about what I was feeling. I wrote asking Jer where he was and if he was trying to communicate with me.

I pretty much spent Saturday and Sunday in various spots outside - wherever the sun was brightest. I just sat in the air, in the warmth. Sometimes out front, sometimes in the backyard depending on my sun to shade ratio. It was an exquisite gift. Sometimes Dawn would come sit with me and we'd just sit side-by-side. Sometimes we'd talk, sometimes we'd just sit. She told me the forecast showed a 100% chance of rain for those days and yet there I sat, in pure sunlight.

I started to get a few texts and Facebook messages saying "Erica? Is it true?" I don't know how word spread so fast; through his siblings maybe? I had told no one, just my family, and now I was getting messages.

As taxing as it felt, I knew I would have to put something out on social media. I did not want people to hear things through the grapevine, I wanted them to hear it straight from me. The big Georgia oak trees caught the breeze from time to time as I tried to write about the death of my husband on that stupid little phone.

"My dear friends... I write with the heaviest of hearts. I have lost my shining light and my warmth when I lost my sweet husband Jeramy Evans on Thursday night. He had trouble breathing and the doctors kept giving him new inhalers telling him it was asthma. Turns out it was a blood clot in his lungs. He was on business in Atlanta and that is where I am now at his sweet sister's house.

Our relationship felt too precious for me to post much about it publicly as though that might jinx it somehow. His presence was a gift to all who had the privilege of spinning in his world for a time - a true example of loving and serving.

The loss is unspeakable and the grief is crushing. He leaves behind a wife and three girls who loved and adored him.

I know we hear it all the time but time is oh so very precious. Put down what you're doing now and go hold your loved ones, tell them how much you love them and how much they mean to you. Thank you my dear friends."

It's strange it hadn't occurred to me until then that the world would need the memo. I hated it as it just made everything so official. The comments started coming in, the messages, the condolences. The 'I'm so sorry for your loss.' Yes, I've tried to come up with something better to say - I'll let you know when I do.

The editor of the Costco magazine contacted me in utter disbelief. "Erica? Is it true? Someone just emailed me and said that your husband passed away!" Our love story came out two weeks before in the February issue. He was apparently contacted by a few different people; he was horrified.

They never ran a follow-up; I didn't want them to. At least in someone's mind, somewhere in this country, we would still be together. Jer would still be here and we would still be very much in love.

Dawn encouraged me to eat a little something. Most of the time I settled on peanut butter pretzels that night we tried pizza. She asked if I'd like to take a hot bath. I love hot baths, I love sinking into that water. Poor Dawn probably needed me to cleanse myself as I'd forgotten that was something adults ought to do.

The master bathtub had a window above it from which I could see those tall oak trees flapping their branches. I stared at them, looking at the shapes they formed. I asked the branches questions and waited for replies. Like move up and down for a 'yes' and side to side for a 'no.' I added more hot water and continued to talk to the trees.

On the brink of tackling another night, at the very moment I thought despair was going to take over, my phone buzzed, I had a message on Facebook from someone I did not know.

"Erica, two years ago I lost my husband unexpectedly and tragically. I know you probably have a wonderful support system around you, but if you EVER would like to connect, I would love to be able to

meet you and share with you about my journey as a widow and I am available to walk with you. Please text me if you want. You are going to be okay. I am praying for you and your kids. You will breathe again."

I felt a jolt of something and comfort at the same time. 'I'll breathe! I'll survive!' prior to that I just wasn't sure. Her message found me at a time I so desperately needed it. I did not personally know anyone whose husband had died young and unexpectedly so it was difficult to know what that looked like or what I should do next.

I suppose that's a check mark in the PRO column for social media and Facebook - how amazing someone I didn't know could find me and drop me a note of encouragement while I sat in Georgia, afraid of the night.

She and I swapped a few Facebook messages - she knew Jer through the adult racquetball league. *"One thing I do want to share, Jeramy came up to me, looked me RIGHT in the eyes and asked me how I was doing. It was only a few months after my husband had died, so most of the racquetballers really didn't know what to do with me. But Jeramy was so sincere and BOLD in his concern for me and I was so touched by his sensitivity to me."*

There he was - there was Jer still looking out for me. I shared the news with my family that I would breathe again and that Jer had a hand in all of this as tears rolled out of my eyes. She sweetly offered to meet with me when I got back to Salt Lake. It's not dramatics or an overstatement to say her messages felt like receiving oxygen. My mantra I repeated frequently for the next while - even still, from time to time: *I will breathe again, I will breathe again, I will breathe again.* I was able to fall asleep for a few hours.

During one of my many hours outside, the phone rang. I'd been expecting a call from the medical examiner with a report on Jer's autopsy. "Hi this is the Country Music Hall of Fame. You're on the waiting list for three tickets to tonight's acoustic Travis Tritt concert do you still want those?"

Huh... Travis Tritt. The Country Music Hall of Fame. Nashville. That's right I was in Nashville. It all came crashing back. The city, the food, the music. The phone call. The drive. I had forgotten all about it. I sat there perplexed - Why was Nashville haunting me? Why couldn't Nashville leave me alone and go away?

"No, our plans have changed," I said to the lady.

"Okay thanks have a nice day and we hope to see you again soon."

I yanked out another tissue, dabbed at my face and sat there. Nashville. I'd been so excited to go and so thrilled to be there. Now it's just a gut-punch that leaves me breathless and weak. I thought about my perfect day alone there - a purely memorable day in every way that ended with such a tragic turn.

Listening for secret messages from the birds, my mind drifted to the concert at The Ryman. The Mother Church. Huh. Church, gospel tunes, feeling something almost indescribable. I began to wonder about the timeline of events; when Jeramy died. I must have been sitting in that concert. I must have been feeling emotional and moved at my personal 'service' while the doctors fought to bring my sweetheart back to life. Was Jeramy there? Did he come visit me before he left? Is that why I felt so much vibrating through my body that night?

I felt goosebumps crawl over my skin as I connected the ethereal dots. The doctors were working to bring Jeramy back but he was with me, saying goodbye to me. Sharing a concert with me. I was convinced of it. All of the music, the pointing to heaven, the original Patsy performing, the love stories of Johnny and June - it was us; it was me. It was Jer. It was his goodbye, orchestrated in a church filled with music, harmonies and stories meant just for me.

Now I slumped in that chair feeling like Jeramy left and he took my other love, music, with him.

The rest of my time at Dawn's moved at a similar pace. She'd bring me coffee in the morning, I'd write, we'd talk, she'd talk to Delta, we'd sit. The funeral plans were moving forward - the funeral would not be until March 10. It would take that long for Jeramy's extensive tissue donation, autopsy, body preparations, and eventual flight home.

Body preparations. What did we want to bury Jeramy in? What should he be wearing? It didn't seem right to have him buried in his work clothes, or work shirts, which is what we had in Atlanta and we couldn't wait until he was back in SLC to have him dressed (I took the funeral home on their word with that one). So I called my mom.

Jer had one suit, we bought it to get married in. I thought of that weeknight we all went suit shopping. I remember how he beamed in the mirror. Now he'd be buried in it. My mom would have to overnight it. His married-in-buried-in suit.

I finally did receive the call from the medical examiner. Dr. Geller called me on Sunday morning. I was sitting outside in the sun thinking I wouldn't hear anything about the autopsy until Monday. "I just finished Jeramy's autopsy," she began. "Deep vein thrombosis..... Blood clots..... Pulmonary Embolism... Totally healthy otherwise.... Tissue samples... Recent air travel... I'm sorry." She was remarkably kind and patient while I sobbed some type of 'this was my person and thank you for taking time and care with him.' I'd speak with her a few more times and would go on to send her supervisor an email saying how outstanding she was. In the world of medicine, when so many of our encounters leave us confused and dismissed, Dr. Geller was just the opposite.

Deep Vein Thrombosis. Naturally I spent countless hours reading about DVTs, emboli and wondering how this possibly went unnoticed. DVTs most commonly form in the legs or pelvis (4-10% occur in the arms). Jeramy was known for his legs;

sounds odd but it's true. He had the strongest, shapeliest legs - shapely in a masculine way. His calves drew envy from every other male, with frequent 'guess you didn't skip leg day huh?' jokes. He just had big strong legs. I pictured him folded into his airplane seat for hours at a time, blood clots forming in those legs while he sat reading a book or watching a show.

That same Sunday, I agreed to join Dawn at her church service. I thought maybe I would hear something uplifting, something I could latch on and hold on to forever. I don't remember what was said. I don't remember the service at all. I only remember the jarring reentry into life. I'd been so secluded at Dawn's for the past few days that I forgot people were still outside living. The normalcy of the interactions, the blasé attitudes with which they approached each other - and certainly their spouses - hurt me in ways I wasn't prepared for.

WHY DO THESE PEOPLE GET MORE TIME?! WHY DO THEY STILL GET TO BE MARRIED?! THEY'RE NOT EVEN HOLDING HANDS - THEY DON'T EVEN LIKE EACH OTHER?! WHY ARE THEY SMILING?! WHAT'S THERE TO SMILE ABOUT?!

The ease and effortless manner these churchgoers moved through life made me ache - made me anxious and antsy. I couldn't leave fast enough.

This 'why them and not me' notion would become quite pronounced for months following Jeramy's death; years even - I still get bouts of it from time to time, though not as frequent. What is it they say? Comparison is the thief of joy - something like that. It became impossible not to look at other humans, other lives and wonder 'why do they still get to be here?' 'Why do they get more time?' 'Why Jer and not him?' 'Why does she get another year with her husband?'

It's not lost on me that those are not the best thoughts an individual can have about one's fellow man but the brain can't help it. Why them and not me?

JER'S BODY

Jeramy and his strong body did extensive tissue donation. He donated his eyes (corneas), his big, hefty leg bones, skin cells, blood vessels and a host of other things I can't think of right now. He was not able to donate organs because the body has to be alive up until they remove the organs (a life support situation, for example). Since Jeramy died and had been gone for 45 minutes, they could not take his organs. Which is a shame - that big, beautiful heart of his should still be loving and giving.

Of course this is a personal decision for every person and, frankly, one that Jer and I never really talked about. A lot of people worry that if they mark 'donor' on their drivers license that doctors won't work as hard to revive them if they end up in the emergency room. Jeramy had 'donor' on his license and they still called next of kin first. They still labored, for 45 minutes, to revive him. I just think it's important to make that note.

Jeramy died on a Thursday night. His body stayed at the hospital where they removed as much tissue as they could. Then he went to the medical examiner for his autopsy then eventually, he found his way to a mortuary in Atlanta where they would prepare him to fly back to Utah.

Dawn and I met with Sparks, a tall, older man with a gentle

southern drawl that I liked. He rattled off the timeline, caskets, working with the mortuary in SLC and when he thought Jeramy's body would be ready - ready for me to see him, "if you think you'll want to."

I knew I wanted to. Rather, I knew I needed to.

Sparks had Jeramy ready for a private, Monday night moment. I both anticipated and dreaded seeing my sweet, hunky in that casket. I'd been to funerals before and I know the bodies in the caskets never look like the person you knew and loved. I just needed a conversation with him mostly.

Monday evening, Dawn and I began the drive to the funeral home; my stomach turned. Sparks met us at the door while someone wheeled Jeramy's body into a private room. We waited. Dawn took a seat. At that moment, the grandfather clock standing in the lobby sang to me. Yes, it was 5 p.m. But of all the songs in the world, of all the tunes a clock can play, it played the tune my late grandpa's doorbell used to play.

We were entranced by Grandpa's doorbell growing up - it played a little song. Ding-dong-ding-dong, dong-ding-dong-ding, down and back up. The best part, rather than having a small white box hanging on the wall with mysterious electronics tucked inside, Grandpa's doorbell was an instrument. It even came with a little mallet - a miniature xylophone on the wall, if you will. In his younger days, Grandpa would lift us up so we could thump the bars on our own, recreating the familiar tune.

I stood in the lobby of the funeral home, ready to say goodbye to my husband and there were Grandpa and Grandma. Comfort washed over me briefly. Many of my happiest childhood memories were spent in their red brick home. I pictured them, I pictured my other wonderful grandparents. It felt like they were saying 'Jeramy is here with us and we're all here with you. We love you and you can do this.' I looked to see if Dawn or Sparks, coming up the hallway, felt the magnitude of the clock strike but they both seemed unfazed. It was just for me.

I nodded to Sparks that I was ready and he led me into a viewing room - the kind that would be filled with mourners during a funeral. Jeramy's casket was on the far side of the room with the top half opened. As I stepped up and looked at my love, Sparks asked if I was okay, told me he didn't want me fainting.

"I'm okay."

"I hope he looks okay, it's been quite a few days and he really donated a lot of tissue which makes it harder," he went on. "We had to use more makeup than we normally like to do and I wasn't sure about his hair."

"Neither was he," I smiled slightly to let Sparks know it was some type of joke.

"Okay well, if you're okay I'll leave you to it."

There was my Jer stuffed inside this box in his married-in/buried-in suit. This robust, larger-than-life, powerfully energetic man all contained. How was it possible?

He didn't look like him, naturally. Sparks gave him a hefty set of jowls from somewhere - almost like a face Jer might pull at a party to make us all laugh. I spent a moment wondering why funeral homes don't let us send some photos so they can see what our person is supposed to look like. How on earth do they mold a face into a cold representation of a living face they have never met?

I finally got to have a conversation with my husband. Naturally, there is no comparing loss and grief, but the inability to have any final conversations, final words with one another - no 'this is what I want you to do' 'just know I love you,' 'here's the Xfinity password' just nothing - was unimaginable.

While Jer was unable to respond to me, I got to talk to him. I touched his hands. I touched his chest. I touched his face, the way I used to. I asked him where he was, if he was around, if he would stay with me. I thanked him for helping me arrive in Atlanta safely that night.

From time to time, I sat down, my hands on his cold hands as they rested on his chest. I laid my head on the side of the casket and just sat with him; in his presence. Then I'd want to see his face so I'd pop back up and look.

I sang to him. Garth Brooks' 'The Dance,' which I've always thought was about a break up but I hear it differently now. I sang the song from our wedding and parts of the first song Jer ever sang to me '...*and when we're old and near the end, we'll go home and start again...*'

I scolded him for leaving, for lying, for telling me he also saw us in 'old people chairs' and that he could 'see us in our 90s'. "Now look at us."

I asked him questions and stared intently at his face waiting for one of those moments the movies so readily dish up - the scenes where something miraculous happens; where there's a sign.

When Jer was here, and the morning was barely creeping in through our bedroom window, not quite light yet, but we were both stirring, I often wanted to tell him I loved him but wasn't quite ready to speak. Not just yet. I'd squeeze his hand or finger three times - a Morse code between the two of us. Squeeze squeeze squeeze. It meant "I love you." Jer would respond with squeeze, squeeze, squeeeeeeeeeeze. Sometimes he'd shake and add lots of movement for emphasis. I'd giggle and he'd pull me in tighter.

Sitting there with him in the room, I squeezed his finger - squeeze squeeze squeeze and I waited. I kept waiting. He just laid there.

I apologized to him for anything I'd ever done that might have been anything less than loving.

What do you say? What does one say when it's their last conversation with a person they love? And when and how do you decide you've said everything you ever needed to say to that person? When do you decide it's time to go?

You don't really. You just end up deciding that after an hour, you've been there long enough, and Dawn was likely ready to be going. There are no other ways to make that decision. It's just time.

I kissed Jeramy. I squeezed his finger three times again and waited. Nothing.

I kissed him again, said goodbye and walked across the large room, looking back at my sweetheart one last time before stepping back into the world.

THE JOURNEY HOME

The Atlanta rain clouds hung low in the sky, a perfect backdrop for the task of getting Jeramy home. Dawn spent countless hours on the phone with Delta making sure the two of us were on a flight together and that Jeramy's body was on our same flight.

I've yet to walk through an airport since, that I don't think of Jeramy, traveling as one of his last tasks on this earth - his time in the airport; when we flew to Cancun together, how much fun we had. I think of me choosing a book to read on that trip to Nashville. Mostly I think of Dawn and myself, entering the airport like two brave soldiers with our heavy task weighing on our shoulders - Jeramy's body somewhere but joining us.

The airport is an interesting place - people from dozens of different time zones, gathered in this spot for now, on their way to another. We tend to associate it with vacations and fun, maybe business. Perhaps it sounds naive to say all the unpleasant tasks that life can dish out and all the unpleasant reasons one would need to travel had never occurred to me before.

Dawn and I navigated our way through family reunions, happy couples, groups of drill teams, a business person or two. The happiness was jarring.

We sat at the gate in silence. Waiting.

As the gate agents began boarding the plane, Dawn and I moved toward the windows where we could see the luggage moving up the conveyor belts into the underbelly of the plane. We waited rather breathlessly looking for my love - looking for visual confirmation that he was on that plane just like Delta said he would be.

Suitcases, car seats, someone's dog but no Jer. We kept watching. Then a large, white rectangular box, all wrapped in plastic was placed on the farther conveyor belt. Dawn and I both saw it at the same time and I burst into tears; I'm sure she did too.

He was right there but felt so far away; he was in that box but he was with us; he cut it close but he was on the plane. I took a picture. I don't know why, it just felt like a moment, felt like I might want proof, felt like it was one of those nanoseconds that come and go in a blink. Who knows why our brains do what they do.

Dawn and I were among the last on the plane. We both had middle seats, I sat directly behind her, and we settled in. I sat between two business men, presumably. No one spoke, thankfully, but they watched me write. I wrote and wrote and wrote all the way home on that plane. I wrote every memory Jeramy and I ever shared - everything I could remember, everything that I thought was fading quickly from my mind; trying to capture it all like leaves in the wind storm.

I don't remember anything else about the flight. I don't remember the length, the snack service, nothing. Just writing. Just my list of memories.

We walked through the airport together and rounded the corner toward baggage claim which, at the old Salt Lake airport, was down an escalator. There at the bottom were our people, our families, those faces a safety net.

There was my mom and one of my sisters, and Dawn could

finally be caught by her own family, to begin her own grieving, not caring for me. We made it and Delta let Dawn know that Jeramy had made it too.

Growing up, my family coined a phrase, "step-by-step, detailed account." We used this term after one of us had been on any kind of trip, referring to the blow-by-blow of the trip. The "On the second day we ate here, we did this, the weather was" etc. Looking back, I think the instances of anyone in our home traveling were fairly few and far between, being there were so many of us, and we all loved living vicariously through the stories. The step-by-step was when souvenirs were presented or maybe some seemingly exotic regional treat. If we were lucky the prints from the 24-hour photo place would be back prior and we might get to look at photos too. We all love the step-by-step (even still).

We left the airport and went to my parents', where I planned to stay until I felt I could muster the strength to go back to my own home. The door opened and there they all were - my Dad, all my siblings and Victoria. Even though we landed late, around 10 p.m. or so, they were there. My family sat waiting for the step-by-step, albeit a much more somber version than any of us were used to.

I wasn't expecting that. I guess I have no idea what I was expecting. But as I received their hugs and shared tears, I sat on the sofa and my gratitude for these people and these faces was immense and it felt good to be home.

JER'S VIEWING

The funeral home had never seen a turnout like what they witnessed for Jer. Hundreds and hundreds of people came, parking in the streets and walking blocks only to wait in line to get in.

I don't remember how long the viewing lasted, two or three hours. And for those two or three hours I stood there by his side, handkerchief in hand (a handkerchief is a brilliant token gift to give, by the way), and I witnessed the impact Jeramy left on this world. I got to watch it play out like a movie almost. Kind of like those movies where they have some type of coming-back-from-the-dead experience and they run around in the final scene acknowledging everybody now that they finally realized these people meant something. It was some other-worldly version of that.

You have to remember, my time with Jer was brief - three years, give or take a month. Most of his life had been lived before I arrived on the scene. While I heard stories, I wasn't really there for any of them.

I don't wish this experience or moment on one soul. But I do think the magnitude of witnessing your person's life, stretching out of the funeral home and into the streets is powerful. I have never been more proud. Proud of my sweetheart and how he treated people. And profoundly grateful and humbled that he chose me.

They came in the droves - neighbors from a decade or more ago. High school friends, football buddies. Women he once dated. Old coworkers, current and new coworkers. His former employees at Wendy's drove at least 30 minutes, still in uniform, to sweetly cry their condolences into my shoulder in Spanish. Some people couldn't speak at all. They would hug me, look at Jer, shake their head and walk away.

The rugby boys Jer coached came by the dozens - big, strappin' Pacific Islanders mostly, dressed in their traditional garb. These young men walked in, heads held high. Some would leave a photo or a token in the casket and pound on Jer's chest saying some chant. They hugged me. Some couldn't speak but some would choke out a word or two about Coach Jer and how he impacted their life.

There were racquetball players and families he friended in the bleachers of his daughter's gymnastics meets.

Some would tell funny anecdotes. Many would tell of a time Jer helped them out of a bind. Throughout the night there would be a few people who came and stood in that line alone with a dogged determination to tell me their story. Jeramy saw them when no one else did. Jeramy was kind when no one else was. Jeramy was a friend to them.

Many would charge up to me and hug me with such meaning and love. The hug was for Jer, I was the next best thing. They wanted to hug him one last time. They wanted to thank him. They wanted to laugh with him. They just wanted one of Jer's hugs.

Some would reach for my hand and hold it the whole length of our chat, not wanting to let go. They slipped me cards. They slipped me essential oils.

Those who interacted with Jer during the last three years, hugged me and thanked me for making his last years such blissful ones. They told me how happy Jer was, how he talked about and bragged about me all the time. How madly in love he was with me. With me. This extraordinary man who lived with such magnitude, was madly in love with me.

I had people show up for me too. People who surprised me. People whose absence surprised me. People who would be instrumental in putting me back together again. These people, these faces, these souls. Their willingness to show up; to look at me at the opening of that dark tunnel and say 'we'll be here... we'll walk with you..." There just aren't words. You guys - we have to show up for each other. Even when we don't know how, even when we don't know what to say. We have to show up for each other.

I hope Jer saw it. I hope he was there. I hope he heard every last word. I hope he knows that the money he willingly spent to pay the rugby dues for someone's son, mattered. That the neighborhood gatherings he hosted mattered. That the free meals he gave employees mattered.

That the smiles, the hugs the laughs, mattered. Deeply.

THE FUNERAL

I remember as a kid the bustle in the home when the family would ready ourselves to be somewhere at the same time. As a family of eight, the house got quite busy - showers, blow dryers, 'where's my fill-in-the-blank.'

The morning of Jeramy's funeral had a melancholy but similar feel. I was still staying at my parents, not quite ready to go back to my own empty house. My sister was also in town.

We all had to be ready. We all had somewhere to be. We were all dreading it.

Jeramy's daughter came over to ride with us, so did my brother, Adam. He came in holding a piece of paper that someone had left under his windshield wipers. It said "Stay Strong." He looked around at the other cars at his apartment to see if they also had notes. A few did, a do-gooder in action, I suppose. Those notes said "cute outfit" or "remember to smile." But on this morning, the note on my brother's car was "Stay strong." We gathered at the front door to say a prayer - a prayer for strength, calm, and peace.

More people came to the viewing prior to the service, then it was time for the family prayer and last look. I remember crying out - I loved this man. I remember kissing him one last time. I remember not a dry eye in the room.

We made our somber march behind the casket into the other room. They expanded that room, opening removable walls and there still wasn't enough space for everyone in attendance. We had people spilling out into the hallways and beyond. The funeral home had never had a larger service.

As we took our seats toward the front, my sis saw one yellow petal fall from the casket flowers, right at our feet. Yellow, Jer's favorite.

A beautiful opening prayer from my sister. A gorgeous musical composition from Jer's sister. Songs sung by dear friends. My brother and dad shared a few words, Jer's sister, two of Jer's friends, his daughter and me.

The second I found out Jeramy died I knew I would need to speak at his funeral. I knew I couldn't sing, but I could certainly speak. I had to. He was an extraordinary husband and I was the only the person who could speak to that. I needed people to know.

I had many come up after and since then, telling me what a beautiful service it was, how moved they were, and that Jeramy made them want to be a better spouse. That's impact.

I don't remember much else, actually, and I've tried. I've tried to remember. I know March 10 was beautifully sunny but the ground was still wet from winter (March 10 is also my grandma's birthday so I liked that it felt special to me).

I don't know, it just felt so strange to be packing up all the photos and flowers and just going home. I remember as a kid when our family would return from an outing - a wedding, grandma's for Christmas - how much we all liked getting home. How much we all liked changing into our comfies, then chatting about the events and such. As we left the funeral home, it felt like that's what we should be doing - Going home to eat some leftover dessert and laugh about something silly that had happened. But this, this was me, my collection of flowers and then what? I was trapped in this existence.

The next day, my siblings came back over to my folks where I was still staying and we ate one of the meals that was brought in. The air and sunlight had the promise of spring. It also happened to be the day of the time change - making the evening beautifully sunny and light. I felt so trapped by my life, by sitting here, by not having a hand to hold, by not being able to go on a walk that night with my sweetheart, just trapped in my own skin. Utterly trapped and suffocating.

AND SO IT BEGINS…

Journal-

There are a trillion firsts with this:

The first holiday - Christmas, birthdays, anniversaries etc.

There are the first bits of news, either good or bad, that you can't wait to share.

The first going places we once went, eating foods we once ate. Hearing jokes you would have found funny.

The first time meeting people who never knew you. The first time seeing the people who did.

First vacations, first time singing. First time watching our shows. First trips to stores, first bowl of popcorn. First time playing UNO.

First dinner at your mom's, first funeral for someone else, first wedding without you on my arm.

First time to wear that dress you loved, first time to not wear my ring.

First time to tell the story.

There are trillion firsts and holidays are just the beginning.

And so began my year of firsts. That iconic and daunting year we all hear so much about - a repeated goodbye over and over. The various holidays are wretched yes, but it's more about the moment to moment existence of a person trying to get through a life they don't recognize anymore and doing so with half of their heart missing. It goes on as a numb blur; nerve endings exposed, everything is both an electric shock and also cannot be felt. You just kind of exist, propped up by the thoughtful deeds, love and support of others.

After the funeral came and went, and the out-of-towners all went home, I decided it was time for me to face going back to my own home. I think there was part of me that worried if I stayed at my folks' any longer, I'd never, ever leave. So this became one of those decisions that doesn't have a 'right' time, you just decide now is the time. I was also trying hard not to add fuel to moments that didn't necessarily need it. The dread is typically always worse than the actual moment.

I hadn't really been back since I left on my trip to Nashville. But, it was time. I told my mom I would be fine and I packed up everything - from my Nashville clothes, to the funeral clothes, plants, and whatever else and went home.

I mostly remember how deafening the quiet was. I stood waiting for the garage door to grind to its stop and once it did, the quiet hurt my ears, and my heart. Everything Jer touched last was where he left it. I wondered if I should just touch and move everything right then; would I regret it; and, as always, does anything have a secret message for me. Deep breath. It was eerie but it was also still home.

There was a note on the door that flowers had been left at the next door neighbor's. They moved in while I'd been away and I hadn't met them yet. I dreaded going over there but thought I could maybe just quickly pick up the flowers without much talking.

They opened the door, I showed them the note. It was clearly a condolence flower display. They said a quick 'we're so sorry' and something about 'we heard he was great' and I hated them. Not because they did anything wrong but because they didn't know Jer. I hated that they could never understand what a terrible loss this really was because they never knew him. And they never would. It was a strange hurt and an even stranger realization that I would spend the rest of my life meeting people who would never know Jeramy.

That weekend, Victoria was supposed to be with her dad but I asked if I could have her for the night because I needed the company. She and I went and got our favorite family pizza. We both quietly tried pretending we were fine until I said "it's not the same, is it?"

Nothing was the same. Sometimes in that first year I wondered if it would be easier to move to a new town; one without so many memories. My brain just played reel after reel of my former life - That's where Jer lived when I'd go over and drink tea, that was his Wendy's, there's where he played racquetball, that's where we bought his married-in-buried-in suit, that's where we had one of our lunch dates, that's where we took evening walks, that's where we went on that double date, that's the turn to his mom's house, that's where we had breakfast burritos, that's our Costco.

Of course, moving away would be the worst as the support system is here. Still, I thought about it.

It happened inside too. That's where Jer made me breakfast, that's where he hung his towel, that's where he got dressed, that's where he sat when we watched our shows, that's where he stood when he greeted me at the door.

It is not an overstatement when I say that humans are remarkable creatures, truly remarkable, that somewhere in that crushing, suffocating grief, we still freaking get up the next day. We are not sure why or where we are going or what the point of any of it is but there we are trying, sometimes with lipstick on.

Getting up and acting like you care about so many unimportant things is the greatest endurance test. It reminds me of shows you watch where the character is on drugs or going through withdrawal and they look down and see their skin moving and crawling - it looks like a bunch of bumps running up and down their arms. That's how it feels. Just a never-ending sense of wanting to crawl out of your own skin. And yet, wanting deep-down to feel happiness again. Wanting pieces of your old self back. I remember feeling like my life had been bumped to a different, but parallel track - like I was in a train car riding next to the train that featured my old life. All of my friends were over there, all the joy and laughter was over there but I was forced to ride over here and yet I could still see - clearly - the life over there. How cruel.

Looking back at photos from that year I can physically remember the hollow buzz/ache I felt in every one of them. No wonder I bristled every time someone commented that it was 'good to see you smile,' as though that smile was some true representation of how I was feeling and the worst was over.

That year brought tumultuous highs and lows. Not highs, I guess, but lows and really lows. I wanted Victoria, who was now 10, to be aware that grieving and crying is okay that it's okay to feel sad. Her evening prayers would include "please help us not feel sad all the time," and all I could do was nod in agreement.

I tried to protect her from the moments of anger or rage that can accompany grief, like the night I ripped Jer's PlayStation from the wall because I couldn't figure out how to watch a DVD with my daughter. I kind of lost it. The whole contraption, all the remotes, all the passwords, I couldn't take it so I ripped it out of the wall. Probably not my best moment.

I also felt really ill-equipped to help Victoria navigate this terrain as I didn't know anything about it myself and I certainly didn't know how to help someone else through it, especially my tender-hearted daughter.

There is a non-profit in Salt Lake City called The Sharing Place, that specializes in helping children through grief and trauma. They do incredible work and their services are so needed.

Victoria and I went for our consultation and as we sat there introducing ourselves I burst into tears. The worker seemed unfazed by it but I would be continually surprised by how close to the surface my emotions were. I pictured a glass filled with water all the way to the top, I was that part where the surface tension is struggling to keep the water from spilling.

I loved what The Sharing Place offered Victoria. It was a gentle, safe place where she was encouraged to talk about Jeramy as she felt led. She is not one to bring up anything unpleasant, I think out of fear of making me sad, and I worried she would wake up at 30 years old with all this pent up emotion still in her system.

She got to share something about him each week, they made crafts, they played games, she got to meet other kids who are also sad but still getting by. On anniversary dates, she got to take in a treat and share a few more things about our person. She took the obituary with his handsome face, often the last stuffed animal he bought her and double-stuffed Oreos - their favorite treat (Jer sneaking her one extra after I said two was enough).

She always came out of there in a better mood than when she went in. So we kept going, the second and fourth Tuesday of the month. The workers said she'll let you know when she's ready to stop coming which happened after about two years.

The work they do is for children of all ages but while they are there, a parent has to remain on-site for the 90 minutes. Sounds easy enough. So I joined the parents in the other room while Victoria went in with her peers.

Each Tuesday we gathered in the room and went around the circle saying our name, who died and how, and we answered a question. Sometimes it was light 'what was your person's favorite food?' Often times much heavier 'What was it like calling people to tell them your person died?' 'How would you spend one more day with your person?'

Stop and think about that one for a moment. How would you spend one more day with your person. Wow. Think of anyone you've loved and lost - how would you spend one more day?

This grief group was something I loved for Victoria but dreaded for myself. It was hard to be thrown in with that much sorrow - suicides, accidents, overdoses - on top of my own sorrow. It was difficult being mixed with people on various levels of their journey. There is no time limit at The Sharing Place, so some parents were new and quite raw in the early stages of their grief and others were years into the slog, making jokes and much lighter in their mood.

I think I went into each week bracing myself; protecting my heart. Perhaps I wasn't open to it. That said, I found myself mulling over a tidbit or a new perspective every time. Someone would say something that would give me a new way of looking at things or a different perspective. Grief group, while I resisted, still ended up being helpful for me in its own way. It gave me things to think about and ponder.

I remember one night early on, one of the women (there with her fiance and her sons after the sudden death of her boys' dad) off-handedly commented "You know we all say 'Your dad or mom would be so proud of you' to our kids. Well your spouses would say that to you too, if they could. They're proud of you and how you're getting through." I thought I was going to burst into tears right then. I hadn't ever thought of that before.

Life is full of the strangest encounters and most absurd moments when you're wearing grief goggles - actually, now that I think about it, it's kind of like wearing virtual reality headset. Have you watched someone wearing one of those? They're in the room but not participating with the rest of the room. And in the goggles, you can hear everyone in the room but you're absorbed in your own moment. Your own reality. That's it. That's the first year.

CLOTHES AND OTHER BELONGINGS

6/25/18

How strange a life interrupted, your sweatpants slung over the footboard.

The reminder notes you left yourself; your keys calmly rest next to your readers.

Everything you last touched; arrested in place, a lifetime gone.

The fabric of your shirts hang limp and still; but I see such life - I leave them hanging.

There is your company shirt I can't part with cause I see you walking in the door from work.

Your turquoise linen button down you posed in on the beach.

I bought you this plaid shirt, a western, hip flare. You wore it to concerts.

A couple of summery Old Navys, Costco button downs, quite a few. And this black silk shirt, a   retro bowling feel, is bursting with life from when you got down on one knee.

Every shirt, even the no-names - I see you in them; I see your frame.

I remember touching your chest in these shirts. I remember conversations, movies, dinners, even a simple walk to the grocery store.

Memories hanging here in these shirts.

I know they're shirts - buttons, collars and sleeves. But to throw them away is tossing my memories.

It's almost as if to touch them is the same as touching you.

So I let them hang, keeping me company.

Your Ragnar jacket, U of U ballcap. Your awesomeness t-shirt, your thin v-neck sweater. your Mr. Happy t-shirt, your lumberjack flannel.

Those were trips to tournaments, summer strolls, picnics & BBQs, sitting in church, the warmest of hugs and jokes with the kids.

And your sun hat is Cancun, it's winning BINGO, it's an anniversary trip. It's sun, love and joy.

So I just keep the pause button pushed. These clothes brought life to my life and bring comfort to my sorrow.

They no longer smell like you but they keep me company.

For now, that will have to do.

A scant few months before Jer died, he and I were binge-watching the TV show, Nashville (freakin' Nashville). There is a couple on the show (Rayna and Deacon, for anyone following along) who just *go* together - always have. They're the couple viewers spent many seasons wanting to get together.

At the risk of offering a spoiler for a show that's been around for a while, Rayna dies leaving Deacon awash in grief. During the gathering at the house, after Rayna's service, Deacon goes upstairs and opens the door to Rayna's closet, and stands there

THE HOPE AT THE END OF THE TUNNEL

looking at all of her clothes hanging there lifeless. Jer and I both went "Ohhhhhhhhh noooooooo....." really seeing this moment along with Deacon. All those outfits, all those memories.

Deacon pauses a beat and collapses to the floor sobbing. Jer and I were crying too. It was unthinkable.

I sat in grief group, discussing our person's belongings - when to go through them, how to and when is it the right time. One lady in our group regretted clearing things out too soon. She thought she was too rash; likely gave away things she might have wanted to keep.

One lady cleared things out in the main living space but kept her husband's office untouched. She said she sometimes went in there to feel him. I pictured a musty, dusty office turned mausoleum - some room at the end of the hallway with a foreboding presence in your own home and I knew I didn't want that for myself.

One person's grandpa chose not to do any of it. His wife passed away unexpectedly 20 years prior and for those 20 years, everything of hers remained. Hair brush where she left it, bras hanging in the closet - untouched. That didn't strike me as a super healthy way to survive two more decades - surviving perhaps, but not thriving.

Turns out there is no *right* time. There's just the time you decide. The time you feel ready to tackle it and frankly, you never really do. You see all this crap differently. Pause your reading for a moment and look around at all of your crap (term used affectionately). I sometimes picture someone else having to come in here and rifle through my belongings. Which would they feel attached to? Which would be hard for them to get rid of? Which would they chuck effortlessly?

"It feels like I'm throwing away a life. We spend time on this planet accumulating things just so someone has to decide what to do with later."

I decided to do what I could do when I felt like I could do it - and trust me some days you do *not* feel like you could do well, anything. I made that my goal during the first year. One day I got rid of Jer's socks, feeling no particular attachment to them, but kept his underwear. One day I got rid of the dress pants Jer wore to work but kept his t-shirts.

I tackled the bulk of his clothes on a Saturday and finally hauled the totes over to Goodwill. The worker came out to the loading area, "Clothes?" "Umm yea…" "Great" He dumped the shirts I'd just folded and took pictures with into great big bins on wheels and rolled them away. Just like that. There went Jer. I paused. I know Jer is here with me and not in that fabric, but still. There goes my man's clothes and the things he wore when we were making memories - happy ones.

Some totes went to his family and I kept a few shirts - the one I bought him, the one he proposed in. A few t-shirts he wore on our breezy weekends together. I'm not sure how long I'll keep them or when I'll feel ready to say goodbye.

I also still have the sunhat he won during a poolside BINGO game in Cancun. He already joined the water volleyball game. We played (and lost) trivia but he had established himself as the life of the party. He hollered "BINGO!," everyone cheered, he ran up to the stand waving his BINGO card in the air. They crowned him winner with a handmade straw hat. He waved hello with the hat to anyone he could see, he posed for photos, he wore it the rest of the trip.

I digress…. But so does your brain when you look at your person's clothing. Your brain just starts playing the highlight reel full of vivid colors and sensations.

I felt so alone, rifling through his belongings. Yes people offered to help but I immediately had visions of having to talk, or pretending to laugh at a joke or a verbal exchange of "what about this?" "where should I put this?" "where does this go?" It was exhausting. I'd rather do it alone.

There's a general grief rule that says don't do anything major for at least a year. No selling or buying homes; no major purchases nothing and I think that makes good sense.

In those first few weeks, I was wrangling getting rid of Jer's car so it wouldn't get towed out of our community. The gal helping me also lost her husband years ago - she was quite young.

Car gal: "You're going to buy something stupid."

Me: "No I'm not."

Car gal: "Yes you will. You're going to buy something stupid."

Me: "No, I don't think I will."

Car gal: "Even if it's something small like a stuffed animal you'll buy it and think 'why did I buy this?'

Me: "No, I'm pretty sure I won't. I'm trying to get rid of things, not accumulate things"

Car gal: "You will, you'll see"

(Please note how exhausted you feel reading that exchange, then add the mind-numbing pain of your spouse dying while trying to endure this conversation. Cruel).

I'm happy to report, I never did buy something stupid - wish I could find her and report back, but I suppose the year rule is there for a reason.

Jeramy had totes and totes of top-of-the-line snowmobiling gear; everything he bought was top of the line. I reached out to some of his snowmobiling friends asking if they could help me price that stuff, I didn't even know what it was. Anxious to have it gone and not hearing back from his friends, I went ahead and made up a price for the entire collection and posted it on KSL.com, our local and likely biggest online marketplace.

A couple of notes: I had never posted anything on KSL before. I knew nothing about how it worked and I knew nothing about snowmobiling.

I picked a completely random price of $300, I think, and I was absolutely bombarded by interested buyers. Worried I was losing a live one, I frantically accepted the very first person who reached out and then the interested buyers started offering more. I *clearly* under-priced my goods. I asked the first guy if he could offer an extra $50 and he was none too kind about it, told me that was pretty crappy of me but grudgingly agreed. I can't even think about how much money I left on the table.

I know you're thinking 'why didn't you Google the items, find the value on that item new for comparison?' or 'why didn't you Google similarly used items of the same thing?' But see that's my point, and it's likely the point of that one-year rule (not that everything is magically better in one year), but the brain can only do so much at any given time. My brain's number one charge was keeping me alive, reminding me to shower and using all of its beautiful autopilot settings to help me do things like drive to work and load the dishwasher. Now that I think of it, it's also during that time, you are forced to handle things like calls to social security, closing of bank accounts, dealing with insurance - it's cruel. My brain could not possibly add the task of 'research all these items you've never seen before to find out how much they're worth.' Insurmountable.

Jer also had all these super nice coolers - big ones - that he used to take to rugby matches. I hauled all of those to a used sporting goods store and I think they gave me $5 each for them. I know, I've since learned those things are pricey and I could have sold them for way more than $5 - and he had several. I just didn't know. I had never bought coolers that size.

Moments like that leave you feeling stupid on top of your sadness and that's not a pleasant combination. People give you that "You did what??!!" expression - both facially and verbally - and it's more than one can handle. 'Yes I did, and I'm glad. I needed them gone and now they are so....' It's awful.

It made me angry. I was angry at the sporting goods guy who I thought could've said 'you know, you could probably sell these online and make a lot more.' I was angry at the neighbor who walked by while I was loading them in my car, asked where I was heading but didn't offer any advice. I was angry at my friend on the phone who admitted later 'yea I was wondering why you were giving those away - they're expensive.' I was angry at Jer for not giving me some kind of 'babe don't give those away' sign. Angry, mad and sad.

Those aren't major things like deciding to buy or sell a house but still, had I waited a year, I might've had the mental capacity to do a little research. There is also no rush and I guess I wish I would have known that too.

I think it's anxious energy - fear of becoming a person who lives in a mausoleum, fear of getting stuck, a desire to not have visual reminder every time you turn around, I don't know, but I felt a need to be moving forward but forward to what?

TWO-MINUTE ROUTINE

I pushed the button on my toothbrush and stood there. The whirring continued while I glanced at the empty second sink - it showed no signs of use.

I looked at my weary face. I looked at my stomach, currently much softer than I prefered, and noted what an eternity two minutes can be.

For months I hit the button and stood there looking at the empty second sink and the empty bed. My bedside lamp seemed to cast a much darker glow than I remember. My simple sleeping space looked meek in the vast king-sized bed, as though it's unwilling or perhaps incapable of claiming more room. The rest of the pillows were stacked in the middle, making a sleeping fort of sorts.

I push the button; the whirring of my electric toothbrush suddenly seems so loud. I feel embarrassed - is it odd I use an electric toothbrush? Does he think so? He's beaming at me but I don't think he is laughing at my toothbrush. He lays sideways across the bed, shirtless, head propped up on his hand. He smiles at me, waiting patiently for the full two minutes my toothbrush requires. It seems like an eternity to keep this man waiting; foam spilling out of my mouth, and my not being able to hear him. But he waits, smiling.

I've never noticed teeth brushing before - such an oddly intimate yet utilitarian moment. I feel so exposed.

"What?" I mumble through the foam. I can't hear him. How terrible. He's trying to chat, I can't hear and, worse, more foam.

He seems amused.

After a few weeks of this new moment in our relationship I begin to feel slightly less on stage but still frustrated that the two minutes seems like a terrible waste of this man's time. I think, deep down, I worry he will grow bored and leave. Certainly there is no way he will lie here waiting two minutes to finish our conversation.

Pretty soon he doesn't.

I push the button, the whirring begins and he starts talking.

"What?" I croak.

But he just smiles. He just gazes lovingly at me and never repeats what he said. "You know I can't hear you," I say as I wipe the water from my mouth.

"I know," he smirks.

Each night, as I spit out my toothpaste I say "Don't say sweet things to me when I can't hear you." But he continues to mumble while I brush. I imagine him saying things like 'I'm going to marry you someday.' I'm pretty sure I'm right.

"Here, lie on the bed," I say to him one night, toothbrush in hand, paste resting precariously.

He gets that boyish glint in his eye, wondering what will come next and stretches out on his back, arms tucked behind his head. I sit down beside him and put the toothbrush in my mouth. As I push the button, I begin to tickle his skin lightly. I run my fingertips over his bare chest, I outline his biceps and shoulders. His eyes roll back in his head, he lets out a pleased sigh, a whimper-sigh of sorts. With each 30-second pulse of the toothbrush my hand roams. Down his legs lightly, up over his boxer-briefs, back to his chest, along his brow, his cheeks.

The toothbrush buzzes three times alerting us both that the two minutes are complete. He groans that it's over, I pat his heart three times for 'I Love You.'

This becomes the way we spend the two minutes.

Each night, I ready my toothbrush, he excitedly climbs onto the bed and stretches out. He groans when the two-minute respite is over as I pat his heart three times. He teases me about shortening the timer.

I tickle him every night during those two minutes. Sometimes he isn't quite ready or maybe he is in the other room and I push the button. He hollers "HEY!" and I hear him thunder through the house and throw himself on the bed. "You owe me an extra 30 seconds!" he says when the three beeps come.

Some nights he falls onto the bed with a weary sigh from a hard day's efforts. I sit beside him and begin our two minutes and can feel the stress evaporate, his body relaxing. Sometimes I close my eyes and memorize the curve of his calves, his thighs, his brow. I pay attention to where his neck and shoulders meet, I imagine his face as I ran my fingers over it.

Other nights I drink in his strong body, looking fully at this man I love who uses all this strength to protect me. Jeramy lies there, feeling my touch and looking boldly and brazenly into my eyes. His earnest gaze searches for my innermost thoughts, wondering if they match his own. Many nights I can hear them: Does she know how much I love her? Does she love me as much? Does she forgive me? Will we make love in a minute?

The toothbrush beeps three times, I pat his heart and he breaks himself from the reverie.

I love touching him. He is pure joy. He is mine. He is lying in bed waiting for me every night. And every single night, no matter what happens throughout the day, we meet for two minutes.

I couldn't look at the second sink anymore. I couldn't look at the bed.

I pushed the button and decided I'd start doing lunges. Two minutes worth of lunges.

Some nights I did squats. Some nights I did lunges. Some nights it was all I could muster to complete the two minutes.

I decided to count that as a work out. The whir of the toothbrush as my accompaniment, the 30-second reminders that I was getting closer, that it was almost over.

My new two-minute routine.

THE MEDIUM

While some folks don't believe in Mediums, my years of wandering around through this landscape wearing a loss-filter, I've yet to meet anyone who's gone through an unexpected loss who didn't try a medium of some sort, at least once.

Mediums, well, any type of communicating-with-the-beyond are usually brought up in hushed tones. Typically a head tilted in, something like "well..... I went to a medium" or "I made an appointment with a medium," and they wait for a reaction.

I love when someone is willing to share, well.. anything, and I love these stories. I'm always interested in how they turn out for people. Mine was... interesting. Full of learnings, yes, but I won't be going back.

My session was gifted to me by a friend who found it helpful after losing her father. I was so eager to go, I immediately booked an appointment, which was about a month after we had buried Jeramy. To say I was still quite raw is a massive understatement. When booking the session, I asked the medium if it would be too soon but she didn't think so.

I don't remember if it was my friend or the medium who said 'you need to make sure you ask your person to be there.

They're very busy where they are and you need to schedule an appointment with them.'

I journaled relentlessly to Jer that we had an appointment and please be there.

"My sweet - Please be there tomorrow at 6 p.m. Please bring your larger than life presence so she knows who she's speaking with. Please bring thoughts that are uniquely you, uniquely me. Uniquely us. Please bring answers to as many of my questions as you can. Please bring thoughts and information that I don't even know I need or want. Please be present, please guide me, please tell me how I can better hear you on my own. Please!"

I remember feeling like it was similar to the "After the Final Rose" night on the ABC series, "The Bachelor." Not trying to make light of anything, but it's sort of the same. You were left behind and you get one more conversation with the person to get all your questions answered. That's what this was for me - one last chance.

This Medium did readings in her home. I arrived early to make sure I'd get every last minute of the session, and sat around the corner in my car, writing a few last thoughts to Jer before it was my time.

She was quite nice and guided me to her reading room upstairs; a comfortable space with two chairs, a rug and a small table with a box of tissues. I don't remember much else. She sat with her legs curled up underneath her, clutching some beads, I sat clutching my journal, a tick nervous.

She set the scene, started some type of music, closed her eyes and 'made the connection.'

I think we envision Mediums and this type of moment the way they're portrayed in movies or in those TV shows where they actually talk to the dead (picture Whoopi in the movie 'Ghost'). And I'm not suggesting that some people don't get that very thing. But I did not.

He showed up at our appointed time. "Your husband is already here," she said. "He shows up in a warm, happy, loving, content way. Where the love just oozes it's just a very comforting and soft and gentle compassionate holding space." That's my guy. But the rest of the session wasn't quite so obvious.

Jer didn't talk like Jer. He didn't sound like Jer. He didn't use phrasing or sayings like Jer did. And, at least in the session, he didn't love like Jer.

Mediums are typically trying to interpret images and other influences that come into view. It's not always perfectly literal; they have to fish around a bit. So, your person on the other side, has to figure out how to communicate to this person they don't know (your Medium) in a way that your Medium understands clearly enough to communicate it to you.

I was expecting to hear and wanting to hear nuggets - one or two things so intensely personal to me that there was no doubt that Jeramy was there and that he saw me. I just remember walking out without any nuggets. None. None of those 'there's no way she could have possibly known that on her own!' type of nuggs.

To be fair, there were a few things that raised my eyebrow. She said "Pride and Ego" which Jer talked about often. So that did catch my ear. She also referenced a 2x4. I said that to Jeramy all the time after his death. Talking out into the air I'd say "Hun you're going to have to use a 2x4 to communicate with me. Be bold."

"He says he hasn't had to use the 2x4 yet because you haven't needed it." And she used a puzzle analogy which Jeramy and I used all the time.

That said, all of those things are actually sayings and analogies the whole world uses. So it didn't feel particularly special to me - Not the way I wanted it to. Not the way I needed it to.

I sat in there for an hour, the music playing softly, the Medium chuckling and laughing with Jer. "He's funny," she said. I had a moment or two of feeling left out. Like the Medium and Jeramy were in on the joke and I was a novice who was asking the simplest and most basic questions.

When you're asking things like 'what was it like when you died?' 'Did you go to your funeral?' and 'Do you miss anything?' and you're asking this to a spirit already on the other side through a Medium who professionally deals with the other side, you end up feeling small and simple - Like a big mortal dope who doesn't understand the Universe or how it works.

Answer I wanted: '…….. when I knew I was dying…. Blah blah … and I thought of you and the girls. I thought about leaving you and how much pain you'd be in. I shouted your name hoping you'd hear, but I didn't have a choice,' Something like that.

Second answer I wanted '…blah blah… my service…. Blah blah…. I saw you speak you were so brave and said such beautiful things. You made me so proud…. blah blah… I loved knowing how loved you felt.'

I spoke at the funeral FOR Jeramy. For the world to know what an amazing husband he was. I wanted to know if he knew that. I wanted to know if he heard it, saw it, was moved by it, if he cared. Did he know how hard that was? He told me to write our story, did he like it?

Third answer I wanted, '…blah….blah…. I miss so many things….. I see you sitting in our chair and I want to be there….. I miss….' well anything would have been nice to hear.

I didn't get those answers.

He was very vague. Yes he was at the service, it was beautiful he was surprised by the tears and love.

He was vague about the night he died. That he was scared but that's about it. Nothing about calling my name (which I'd always envisioned when I pictured him leaving this earth, "Ericaaaaaaaa!")

But the real zinger was - "He says, he doesn't miss things in the way you do. He's completely full."

Ouch.

When you have lost someone you love a scant six weeks prior, to hear 'they don't miss you' is crushing. I know, I know and I get it. It's different there, they don't have the physicality and all the rest of it but to that person, sitting so small and meek in the chair, clutching a journal, with a wadded up tissue, it's crushing.

He's completely full.

She went on.

"That doesn't mean he doesn't understand the depth of what you're going through." The. Hell. He. Does.

She chuckled back and forth with him a few times, "Yea he's saying he knew you weren't going to like this."

She told me this was my choice, that Jer and I planned it before we came down, "you are the one that wanted to complete the full earth journey." Impossible.

"There is more that you had planned to do with your life that couldn't happen with him in it - Something you were going to do but it's so far removed from where you were going with him."

I slumped in my chair a bit as she told me I was going to be on this earth for a long time (which sounded torturous to me at the time) and that I'd have a strange attraction to birds, (not my favorite). "Birds walking with you, near you but what's important is hearing their chirping - hearing that vibration. Listening for messages in their chirps."

She also told me I was clairaudient - frankly, a word I had to look up when I got home. "You have the ability to hear things and you've had it since you were a little kid." She told me I need to practice sitting in the dark and listening.

So that's it? Great. Sit in the dark, listening for who knows what and watch out for birds. I don't even like birds.

"Grief is an every moment event," she said. (Which the modern-day me, reading the transcript, likes - Because it is). "But we promise it gets easier. Your life will get better, we promise."

We? Now they're a 'we'?

My Jeramy, my sweetheart, sounded flip and casual, almost mocking even. Just chuckling, cracking jokes, saying he doesn't miss things but that he knows what it's like down here. No Jeramy, no you don't know what it's like down here. You don't at all.

I left feeling quite empty and alone - abandoned by my sweetest friend who I now envisioned rolling around in the golden fields of heaven with nary a care in the world, while I was slogging through, barely surviving down here on earth. I was angry and hurt.

Back to Mediums - I think they can be helpful and I understand the need for answers or *some* type of closure. But I wish I'd given myself time. I wish I waited a year so that my brain wasn't working so hard just keeping me alive. I should have waited until the numbness wore off a bit - maybe I would have been more open to hearing things like 'you chose this' and 'he doesn't miss you like that.'

I needed more than six weeks to begin trying to visualize the vastness of the Universe and my place in it.

One important note for those considering some type of communication with the other side: You are allowing someone into to your heart and brain at your most vulnerable time. Your MOST vulnerable. All of your walls of protection are down, you have no defenses - it's just you sitting there, with your heart in your hands, letting someone else poke around in there to see what they can find.

That's not how they view it, of course, but it's a good visual - if you're in pain and seeking answers in that space, you have to decide if now is the best time to let someone poke and prod your aching heart. Perhaps, right now, your poor heart has been through enough.

GARAGES AND CHOICES

I stumble upon a post-it note: "I love you - you're the most amazing person I've ever known." I root through the box, find the rest of Jer's hidden notes, and stack them in a 'keep' pile.

There is a personalized mouse pad - filled with photos of vacations, that Valentine's scavenger hunt and home-cooked meals. There are the CDs I burned for him that are nostalgic enough to put in the 'keep' pile. I can't remember the last time I listened to music on CD but still, it seems too abrupt to just chuck them.

Box by box, I stop to look at my progress.

This is not the first time I've stood over a box of a man's belongings, cold from garage temperatures and, one-by-one, decided what to do with things, stuff. Each item in every tote, and every box, in a garage-full of life, relationships and choices.

That was a different set of circumstances all together - divorce - painful, in different ways, but also its own grieving process.

That clean-out day was November, the start of the winter season setting in and a deadline - an out-of-the-house / out-of-the-storage unit / divorce finalization deadline bearing down. I needed to be out of the storage unit by the end of the week and it had been a dumping ground for the stuff I didn't want to deal with, the leftover things he didn't want to deal with and stuff he never claimed as his.

I took the day to tackle the project. Box by box, I rooted through memories - photos of the happier times, photos of the times I fake smiled for the camera. Photos of the times he did.

It was a heavy day. It was a day of facing one's choices - my choices - of wondering what went wrong, and why. What could I have done differently, why he didn't seem to care more.

I rifled through the boxes full of crap pulled from my closet, another box full of stuff he had dumped from the old garage and a duffel bag full of shoes I thought I'd wear on all the nights we went out. They hadn't been worn. I tossed them in a 'chuck' pile and moved on. Purses, hiking boots, books - donate box.

In the next box sat kitchen stuff - my decorative dessert plates - a Hawaiian set and one themed with shoes. They'd only been used on one random night we had people over - my friends. The wet bar set I was sure would get lots of use, sat dusty in the same box.

I kept them, hopeful for a new life.

My nose ran most of the day; I wished I'd worn gloves. I hauled boxes to the dumpster. I condensed boxes. I made 'keep' boxes.

All day long, I worked in the dreary, damp November day, revisiting my mistakes - his too.

As I looked through these boxes wondering if any of it mattered, I was struck by the song playing from the phone in the back pocket of my grungy jeans - "You Matter to Me," from the Broadway musical, "Waitress." I put it on repeat. I learned the words.

Because you matter to me

Simple and plain and not much to ask from somebody.

You matter to me

I promise you do, you, you matter too.

I promise you do, you see?

You matter to me.

The storage unit had been condensed to one small keep pile, and a few 'you didn't mean to drop this off here' boxes. The rest was empty. Sorted, cleared and gone. My nails were broken, my body ached, my nose was still running.

With a pounding head and tired joints, I closed the door and stiffly made my way back to my apartment.

I stood in the living room in my filthy jeans and ratty sweatshirt, holding the meager box of the few things I deemed worthy of saving, wondering where to set it.

My phone was still on repeat in my back pocket when Jer, still a boyfriend at the time, walked in after his long day of work. The November sun set long ago; it was dark and cold.

One quick look at me, he said nothing. He took the box from my hands, set it aside and gave me a hug. The kind of hug they talk about in the song - *".... they want to hold you for 20 minutes straight. They don't pull away, they don't look at your face and they don't try to kiss you. They just hold on tight without an ounce of selfishness to it."*

He wrapped me up in his arms, weary from their own day, and held on tight. I choked back tears, tried to find words to say to make this seem normal; less dire; less desperate, less painful, less sad. But I couldn't. I couldn't find words.

As the song played, I felt his arms - his steady embrace of support, his love, his deeply embedded desire to patch all the holes in my heart with this hug and we swayed gently to the music till soon we were tenderly dancing, but not speaking.

We swayed, temple to temple, my breaths hitched and unsteady, until I realized that he knew. He had been there. He had rifled through his own storage units of past lives, old photos of choices and decisions that didn't turn out as planned, and he had likely sorted through his own box of decorative plates he thought he'd use one time or another but didn't. Yes this man wrapped me up like this because he cared, but also because he had lived this day - this day of sorting and choosing - and he knew the pain.

Peace washed over me not only because of the hug and the impromptu silent dance, but because I was grateful that he wasn't bothered by my sadness. He knew it was remorse and regret from another lifetime, he knew it wasn't meant for him and didn't reflect on our current chapter together. He just 'got it;' he understood - no explanation required.

I find another stack of CDs: "Waitress - for my love," I look at the CD I burned for him and pause. I remember the quiet dance that night; nothing said, nothing spoken - all sadness understood and communicated through silent tears and a warm embrace. How does one make a decision to chuck something so meaningless on the surface but impossibly meaningful in the heart?

It feels exhausting and I wonder why I was, once again, having to stand here rifling through boxes, and figuring out what to do with the contents. I donate various items, sold others, and wonder about keeping some. His pile of love notes got higher, my pile of things to chuck got higher.

I open the box of the decorative plates and, thinking about how many times they've stared up at me from inside a box, virtually unused, put them in the donate pile once and for all.

In the corner sits his bike. I reminisce about his company fitness challenge - how committed he was to winning, me waiting in the driveway for him to bike around the corner for a sip of my drink and a kiss - now the bike sits, almost slumped, in the corner of the garage with two flat tires and a broken spoke.

It's then that my ex-husband stops by to drop off Victoria. I ask his opinion on the bike. He pulls it out, bounces it on its tires a few times, crouches down to look at the gears and chain and offers to help me spiff it up in order to sell.

I feel stupid in this full-circle moment. Asking my ex-husband to help me sell the bike of the husband who died. I wonder if he notices this moment too. If he does, he doesn't let on. He is just quietly sweet about it. I love him for that.

DOUBLE THE GRIEF

Naturally I swore I would never sing again. Ever. There was no joy in my life anymore - I knew there never would be and singing had always been such a joyful activity.

I think part of it was some type of punishment for someone? The world? God? Some type of dramatic 'then I'll never sing again!' throwing myself on the bed or some type of grand gesture like that.

In rereading journal entries, I noted that people would comment 'I don't hear you sing anymore.' 'Nope. And you won't.' Rather than trying to be dramatic, I think it became my version of wearing black; an outward manifestation of my sadness.

The other part of it was this notion of knowing nothing would ever be the same and I knew that. While logically and mathematically I knew I could sing if I wanted, I felt so fundamentally different - from the inside out - it was inconceivable that I would feel like myself enough to sing, ever again.

So I didn't.

And I wouldn't.

I drove in silence in the car; the music too jarring for my soul.

I felt absolutely betrayed by God, by the Universe, by any other influence that was ever present in my life. Perhaps betrayed by music? It just felt so inexplicably unfair - why Jer? And why music?? Why did it have to happen while I was on a music trek? Why did it have to happen while I was enjoying Nashville, the Ryman, Patsy and country music?

I even felt betrayed by Jer, as though he had a choice. Why now? Why this trip? How could you?

I've taken a lot of mundane trips in my day. I've even taken a lot of great trips that weren't as personally meaningful as this trip to Nashville and THAT'S when this happened!? It just felt like a double whammy, like I'd lost my two great loves: Jeramy and music.

I still felt like the butt of a huge cosmic joke as the mentions of Nashville in my daily life increased dramatically. It wasn't just the country music station - It was the new guy at the ad agency just moved from Nashville; it was multiple friends of mine all randomly trekking to Nashville for whatever reason; it was a scene in a random show taking place in Nashville. It was exhausting and it was constant.

Numerous times I had to interact with people about that town, forced to act like whatever they were telling me was neat. Numerous times it was a deeply painful reminder. I unfollowed anything Patsy Cline on social media. I unsubscribed from the Nashville email sent through the city's chamber of commerce. I was done with all of it.

The perennial challenge for me though: I don't know how to process anything, without music. I do not know how to navigate through the world without experiencing music, finding songs that match what I'm feeling, attaching music to my life and what is happening. So how was I to navigate the biggest challenge of them all, without my lifetime companion? Music had always been there for me.

I drove around in silence for a while until I started to feel the need for my old companion. I turned on the car radio and luckily Sirius Satellite radio offers every genre. I certainly wasn't ready for any type of country so I settled on classical. Something soothing, something gentle. Music that did not yearn to be sung. It took the edge off a bit and opened me up to consider getting back together with music; a jilted lover considering reconciliation.

This went on for a while, Mozart and me. I began to feel ready to accept another music apology and I started dabbling in other genres, trying 70s and 80s for a time. Sirius has a range of channels that begin roughly at 50 and works their way up to 56 or 58, featuring various types of country, Blue Grass, modern country, Willie's Roadhouse, Prime Country so on and so forth.

That has always been my preferred range. I just move the dial back and forth from 50 to 60. Every once in a while I'll pop over to Frank Sinatra, but primarily I just stay in this range. Initially, I decided I could try the new music country station and maybe some bluegrass since I didn't have any memories associated with those. I'd sit on 56 for a while and then click really fast up through the others until I got to 60. I knew I could not land on Willie's Roadhouse as the odds were highest that station would play not just Patsy, but any of the music I heard that night at the Ryman. I also knew the Gatlin Brothers would be played on Prime Country. So I skipped that station too.

I spent large chunks of my quiet nights playing sad songs on the piano, thank you Beethoven. I tried singing a few sad songs but didn't have the energy to eke out more than a few notes. Very tricky of music to present itself that way so I wouldn't recognize it was trying to reconcile.

While I was working hard to avoid music, music was spinning its own web of magic to find me and, while I didn't know it at the time, would be (and continues to be) integral to my healing.

My visit to the medium packed a wallop. Her saying Jeramy giggled and told me he 'knows what it's like down here' angered me. I felt mocked, I felt a fool, I felt like he had truly left me - not died but left me. Left me and was having such a great time up there; he now had the full story so he wasn't worried about me anymore. It was painful.

Do you remember "Where in the World is Carmen San Diego?" (bear with me here). The theme song was sung by the group Rockapella - An all male acoustic singing group, they actually have a lot of albums but are, perhaps sadly, best known for the theme song.

I hadn't listened to Rockapella for years. Years. Decades. Maybe since high school or college?

And yet, through the hurt of the medium, an old Rockapella song, "Don't Tell Me You Do" cropped up - this is how music works for me - it's like my brain is my own librarian and is constantly thinking 'hmm I know a song that goes with that, here let me find it.' Suddenly I'm singing a song I've not heard since what, 1998? Then I need to look it up, remind myself of a few lyrics, but most importantly, I need to sing it. I need to sing the words, I need to feel them move over my vocal cords.

"So you say you've been here,

You know me,

You really understand

You've felt, the way I feel.

Sugar let me say

I don't think you even have a clue, of how you've blown my life apart

Honey you got no idea…

Don't tell me that cry in your sleep each night

Don't say you spend each hour wondering what wasn't right.

Do you stare into the mirror thinking what is it you should change?

Do you wake up every morning reaching over to find you ain't there and you ain't coming back?

You cannot know how this feels,

Don't tell me you do."

I needed to sing these words. I needed Jeramy, wherever he was, to hear me say 'you have no idea what it's like down here doing this all alone. You have no idea and don't tell me you do.'

My first try singing again wasn't from joy. It was sorrow, anger, pain and confusion. I tried to eke out 'don't tell me that you cry in your sleep each night' in the shower. It came slowly and tentatively - scared of my own voice almost.

I could feel my vocal cords moving, like an old friend and that also made me cry. My voice was still there, waiting for me.

I played that song over and over and when I could, I'd eke out the chorus while tears poured from my eyes..... *"You cannot know how this feels. Don't tell me you do."*

Trying to ease my pain a bit, my brain the librarian, had a thought 'heeeeey, wait a minute - I remember a song, let me find it....' And just like that, I went from singing Rockapella's "Don't Tell Me You Do" to singing "A Thousand Winds That Blow," by Steve Wariner, a popular country music singer in the 80s.

Here's where it gets interesting - I heard the song not long before Jer died. I'm not sure where I heard it but I made a mental note 'that'd be a good song to sing at a funeral.' I even pulled out my phone and jotted it down. I get asked to sing at funerals from time to time and, understandably, the family often doesn't know what song they would like sung, so I have found it helpful to have a few suggestions in my back pocket. I shake my head at me thinking 'that'd be a good song to sing at a funeral.'

It begins *"Hold your head up and don't you cry*

When I'm called home and must leave..." It's beautiful.

But the chorus is what my brain found for me:

"I'll be the sunshine in your morning that warms your pretty face.

That bluebird on your mailbox and the soft autumn rain.

I'll be those children in the winter making angels in the snow

I will be a thousand winds that blow."

I played the song and there were my goosebumps. *"I'll be the sunshine in your morning that warms your pretty face."* There he was. That was Jer. He wasn't laughing at me. He wasn't mocking me. He was right here. He always was my sunshine - bold, bright, warm, all encompassing - and now he's using it, musically, to remind me. In that one sentence he's telling me he's here and he's bright. He's telling me he's bringing me warmth. And he's calling me pretty. That's Jer.

JUNE JOURNAL

I wonder what you'd say to me if you could.

If you could flop here on this bed, and say something to me, what would it be?

Would you tell me that you miss me?

Would you tell me that you're proud?

Would you tell me you were hugging me all those night I cried out loud?

Would you tell me that you miss my scent and the gusto of my laugh?

Would you say you heart was broken leaving me the way you had?

Do you ever wish for one more talk, soft and loving like I do?

Don't tell me you're fulfilled, my heart knows that can't be true.

I imagine that you watch me proud admiring my strength.

That when I think I can't go on, you're there each step of the way.

My sweet, I wonder what you'd say to me, if you could.

And maybe you're trying... I wish that you would.

LIKE AN ANGEL

My friends and I perused the many booths at the Salt Lake Arts Festival - the big annual art extravaganza held downtown every year. The whole city flocks to it. Food trucks, cold beer, lots of artisans from ballet dancers to pottery makers and everything in between. They have live performances and an arts area for the kids. The summer night air is beautiful and you have a good chance of running into people you know. It's just a fun night out.

One particular booth had a lot of jewelry made from various stones, which I love. I wandered in, giving a casual glance at the rings under the plexiglass but not seeing anything that struck my fancy.

My friends caught my eye and motioned they were moving on. As I was leaving I turned to the worker and said "Hey, do you know what this stone is?" showing him the beautiful dark green stone ring we bought in Cancun because I needed a reminder of Jer, his eyes and that trip.

"Looks like seraphinite to me," he said.

I made a mental note to look that up when I got home, thanked him and turned to leave. "Like an angel" he hollered after me. I felt a rush through me.

"What?"

"Angelic, seraphim" he said.

Huh.... the ring I chose was seraphinite. I smiled to myself. I couldn't wait to get home.

I looked up the stone and felt another wave of whatever that is. Seraphinite's properties include: "Strong energy to contact the angelic realm. Meditating with this you may discover you connect with the angelic realm. Aids contact with nature / spirits. Stimulates clairaudient & clairvoyant abilities."

The Medium had also mentioned being clairaudient. I immediately contacted my new-agey friend to tell her. She wasn't entirely sure the guy was right cause of this and that, but I didn't care.

What are the odds that of all the stones in the world and all the jewelry booths at the festival, that I'd pick the one with the guy who shouted after me "Like an angel!"

It was for me.

WHEN I CRY

My journaling had morphed into me trying to make my sadness more interesting. I worried when I died, I would leave behind volumes of journals of me saying "I'm so sad; I'm so lonely; I miss you; I cried today; Were you here today?; I'm so sad."

I am struck by the notion that my own sadness was boring to me. As I went back and read my journals, I have thought 'oh here I am again, still sad.' This is how others often react to those of us moving through unspeakable sadness and that's when the 'shouldn't you be over this by now' commentary comes in. And yet, the me writing those words - that was all I could feel at the time.

I started dabbling in poetry and song lyrics - both rudimentary at best but I liked it. I liked that brain flex. It forced me to find structure for the pain. Not that it helped me make sense of it, but it did encourage me to find other words, words that rhymed, ways of saying things with new color.

I began with the song I sang at our wedding, "I Hope You're the End of My Story." There were times I wondered if I'd picked a more standard love song would he still be here? Had I jinxed it? He wasn't the end of my story. If the Medium was right, I still had decades left down here - enough chapters to make their own book. In fact, should I live to be 90 Jer would be a really small chapter. He will actually be a really small chapter no matter how long I live, if I'm being perfectly honest.

At any rate, I wrote an addendum verse to that song. I remember feeling like the words came easy and I wondered if the Pistol Annies would like to add them to their own song some day.

"Life's turns can be unexpected

It's twists will bring you down to your knees.

You'll question the reason, why you're so neglected

Your future is not guaranteed.

You were the best part of my story

You were the best thing that I chose

And I'll always wonder why you went before me

And why it was your time to go."

By July of that year, I had written my own song, at least the lyrics anyway. I had verses and a chorus. It rhymed, it told a story; I liked it. I journaled, *"I created something for the world today that didn't exist before."* I mean, I'd written a song - How magical!

"Good morning my love, I still say every day.

I greet you when I walk through the door.

I still ask how you're doing and I ask what you think,

And I tell you what my day has in store.

I tell you about so-and-so

And I ask if you've heard.

Sometimes I share a chuckle or two.

I still imagine you like what I'm wearing today,

And I smile and say 'it'll have to do.'

Chorus

But I can't see your face or the warmth in your eyes

And I can't feel your hand laced in mine.

And I can't feel the want in your kisses and night,

And I can't turn to you when I cry.

Verse

I set the coffee, do dishes and watch a quick show,

Head upstairs and turn out the lights.

I stack all the pillows on your side of the bed,

To cuddle against through the night.

Chorus -"

I ordered manuscript paper and then sat down at the piano trying to boot up my music theory class from high school (music theory is hard guys - it's the math part of music and it's tough). It was a rough, rough start. No one else could take what I'd written and play or sing the song, it's not at all accurate. But it was enough for me to feel like I'd at least gotten it on paper.

I loved the process. I loved everything about it except trying to put it on paper. I wondered if a more forgiving instrument, like the guitar, would allow me to write my own songs, me making up melodies while I strummed.

Good old Amazon had Betty (named after Jer's car, Betty White), a guitar case, replacement strings, four picks, a capo and a tuner on my doorstep in two days. I instantly fell in love with it.

I loved sitting with it, I loved learning chords, I loved watching YouTube videos, practicing my finger placement. I loved telling my brother, who also plays guitar, about my progress.

I downloaded the Guitar Tabs app and found the collection of songs I could play was growing with each new chord I learned. Country songs can be quite easy to play so I found myself, slowly, reuniting with my old companion.

Guitar, for me, cannot be played without singing along. Hesitantly and tentatively, almost as if singing would tell the universe that I was okay with what happened, I sang while playing. Willie Nelson tunes, the song I sang at our wedding (which I rarely dare to play), songs from The Judds, Randy Travis, Hank Williams.

Music was working to soothe my feelings. I was sampling the country music stations in the car as well. Sometimes I skipped songs, but mostly I was working to let myself stop and reflect. Sometimes I wondered if I could learn to play certain songs or I would take photos of the screen in my car to remind myself to look up that song later.

Guitar was not only helping me fill my free time, but also helping me make sense of sadness. It was actively creating a space for me to pause, sit and feel my sadness. I know that might not sound like a lot of fun, but it was profoundly helpful on the path to healing and it was disguised as learning. And, rather sneakily, bringing music right back where it belongs - nestled against my heart.

JULY JOURNAL

I don't smile to make you feel better,
actually, maybe I do.
I don't smile to make myself feel better,
well maybe I do that too.
The pain and grief are too much to handle,
No one knows what to do with it.
They stare they shuffle they glance away,
wondering why I have to be so true with it.
So I smile cause it seems the easier way.
I smile, cause no one knows what to say.
I smile cause it puts them at ease,
It's simple.
I smile cause I don't what else to do.
The awkward discomfort hangs in the air with every person I see.
And I stand there wishing they'd not search for despair
and instead just try to see me.

STONE SLAB

I love my husband's headstone.

Isn't that a ridiculous sentence?

I know it's painfully absurd but the design of his headstone is one of the decisions I really feel like I got right.

I remember sitting at Dawn's house realizing we'd have to pick out a cemetery - a resting spot - for my man and I wailed. It was unspeakable pain.

His parents offered to have him buried where some of their other family members rest - one of the oldest cemeteries in Salt Lake City. It has a lovely view, one set of my own grandparents are there as well. But it's more of a creepy cemetery, if that makes sense. It's very old, very uneven and sits on the mountain side. I couldn't envision sitting there for any length of time.

I knew I wanted him across the valley at the cemetery where my other grandparents rest. Having visited on Memorial Days it feels brighter, more open, and it's right at the bottom of the Wasatch Mountains. How lovely, I've always thought, to get to lie there and stare at those beauties every day.

Looking back, I can tell I was making these choices knowing I would want to go visit Jer and sit with him. I've since learned a lot of people don't. They put their person in the ground, put a slab of granite over their head and never go back.

A big crew of us went to the cemetery to select a resting spot. It was my family and Jer's family (which is a lot of us). They took us in a waiting room and said "Chris asked to work on this project - he'll be right in." In walked Chris, a big, bold presence with a warm smile. His first story? He knew Jer! He worked with Jer for a time selling windows - they'd even road tripped to Idaho a few times making sales calls.

I was immediately comforted by the thought that someone who knew and loved Jer was helping us find the perfect spot. I wanted to have him close to my grandparents but those plots were filling quickly and were pricier.

Chris took us out to the newer section and we found the right spot, close to another young dad, stunning views of the mountains with young trees planted nearby which will soon provide more shade. It's the perfect resting spot, if there is a such a thing.

Have you ever designed a headstone? Have you ever given an ounce of thought or energy to what you'd like etched in granite to encompass all that you are? All that you were?

I'm making this part easy for my family: I want music notes. And maybe something like "Erica loved her family" "Victoria is her greatest joy" Something like that. That's it.

Hmm... now that I think about it - should we pick our own etchings or should our loved ones get that honor?

I'll tell you what I know and what I learned through that process.

Lesson one: Don't pick too soon.

Jer died on March 1, and was buried on the 10th. I remember the funeral guys saying "If you want the headstone in by Memorial Day you need to order it this week."

I didn't want to. Couldn't if I had wanted to. The thought of burying Jer was so taxing, trying to process what kind of stone slab I wanted was preposterous.

So he had nothing for Memorial Day but he didn't mind; neither did we. We visited him anyway.

Slowly, over the next few months, during my cemetery visits, I began to notice the cemetery. I began to notice how insignificant Jer's grave looked. A 2" by 2" plastic marker screwed into the ground. That was it; that was all he had. All around me were flowers, and grandiose names carved in stone; photos; poems; even a recipe.

I made numerous journal entries apologizing to Jer for how lacking this display was - that people would wander by and think 'who's this unimportant person? He must not have been that neat - no wonder no one cares about him.'

Long about July, I couldn't take it anymore; I needed Jeramy to have significance.

I made an appointment and took the afternoon off work. I met with the funeral workers (I'm sure they have a more accurate name) and they took me into a room with a bunch of granite slabs hanging on the wall. There were urns, above ground headstones and flat headstones. There were small headstones for babies (God forbid) double headstones and various sized single headstones.

Size and color were the first two decisions. Needing Jeramy to have significance, I knew I'd be bothered during every visit if his headstone was smaller than the neighboring headstone. So I got the bigger size.

Lesson two: Don't scrimp.

When making headstone decision, splurge for what you feel you'll enjoy during visits. Don't scrimp on this one. That is, of course, unless you feel you won't be visiting. Those expensive caskets, you never see those - It's in the ground, encased in concrete, never to be seen again. But this headstone is seen by everyone who wanders by and most importantly by me (you) every time I go. I sit and I stare at that headstone. It's worth putting in thought and it's worth getting right.

They put this binder in front of me full of line sketches of all the possible suggestions one could get on a headstone. Everything from angels and crosses, to motorcycles and snakes, even rats. Deer drinking from lakes to trains; all kinds of birds and flowers to electric guitars or RVs. There are binders of them. I even chuckled a few times and said "Rats and snakes? Do people want rats on their headstone?" The worker said "You'd be surprised. Sometimes what happens is people pick too soon" (see lesson one). "They have a dream about their person and maybe there was a snake in the dream. Then they sit here and think that dream meant something and they put a snake on their headstone."

See the error? That slab of granite is going to be there for a long, long time. You hate to have a snake on there as a rash decision. If your person was a herpetologist, then perhaps it might make sense, otherwise, best to let your brain have a chance to figure out what the hell happened first.

7/11/18

Oh my sweet… How do I capture the essence of you in some etching in granite? How do people do this - is this what we all come down to? Some stick etching /one or two symbols to communicate to the world what the person was or meant?

I tried to see if they could maybe do a sunset - we love them so much. But it looks more like a sunrise and doesn't feel like you.

Gin & Tonics? Our double camp chair? Mimosas? Guac?

What could possibly capture all that is you?

How can a trivial stick etching showcase your warmth, your charisma, your charm? Your glorious hugs, your beaming smile?

Your hearty laugh, your quick wit, your work ethic? Your sweet kiss, your tender touch, your unmitigated desire to serve? How do I capture all your big, bold, breathless love in granite?

It all seems so insignificant, doesn't it?

Here's a football and rugby ball, 'loving husband.' Here's a 'U' - best dad.

What about NASCAR insignia? Racquetball? Snowmobiling?

Your mantra was love, your mission, service, but you can't etch those.

Here lies:

"If it's not awesome, it's not good enough"

"Comin' in hot"

"Wasting time on others"

"He loved all others above himself"

"We'll go home and start again"

"He showed love through service."

"My sweetest friend"

"I will be a thousand winds that blow"

"I freaking love you"

"A true renegade" or "my sweet renegade"

"I'll be loving you always"

Should we rattle off all of your titles? 'Husband, dad, son, brother, uncle, friend."

What about 'all around best'

'I can't wait to see you again… it's only a matter of time."

Flowers, angels, weeping angels.

I'm not a designer hun. I don't know how to do this. Please, please communicate with me what you want on your headstone.

Hearts should be on there. And I think I'd love your handsome face to gaze back at me each time I'm there.

Sigh… my love… granite etchings don't do you justice. Yours really should come with a QR code so folks could scan and read more about you.

Tell me what you want

OXOX

7/19/18

My love, you wrote so many beautiful notes to me. I have a marvelous collection from which to choose. I thought it might be fun to see if they could etch your writing on your headstone.

What do you think of that? I don't know - I've never designed one before.

But your beautiful sweet notes - what an extraordinary collection for me to have. You love me so much. I hope you felt as much in your last days, hours, moments.

Here's the clincher- in this world of computer graphics, amazing 3D capabilities, artificial intelligence, virtual reality, there is nothing - no such capability - for showing a grieving person what the headstone they're designing will look like. Nothing. Nada. You just get a line drawing confirmation that this is what you want.

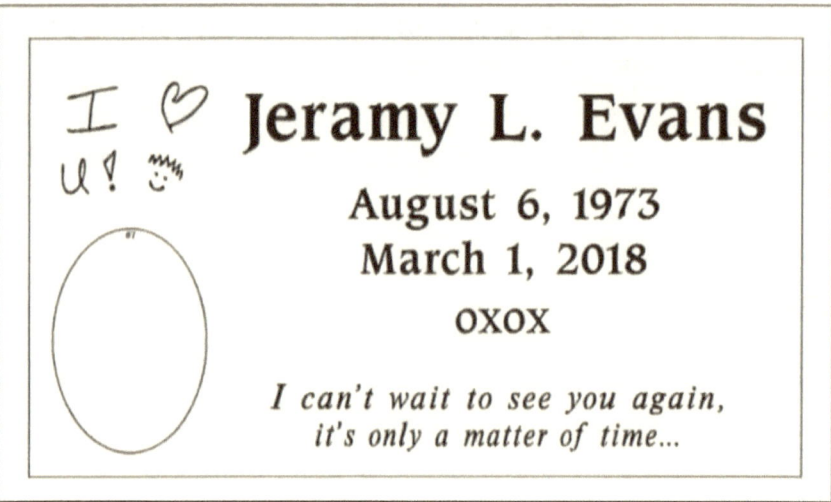

How do you know if you'll like it? What if you hate the size of the photo? What if you don't like the border? What if it's too crowded - you're just depending on black lines on a white paper and your good ol' imagination. Preposterous. I promise if this were a more competitive industry, and it weren't a purchase people *had* to make, you would have all sorts of renderings to help you design and decide just like on HGTV (there's an idea: CemTV).

Luckily, I have a friend with some Photoshop skills who quickly slapped together a few renderings. This helped me decide between gray granite (did that look better with his photo?), or the warmer granite with a bit of red hint to it (I'm sure there's a technical name that I paid for).

I was pleased with the design. I designed the whole thing - and remember, I'm not a designer - but every single line on that headstone is meaningful and has a reason and story behind it. Every one of them.

Obviously his name and dates are on there - which I still check for accuracy every time I visit. I also included his handsome photo; yes it was extra but I didn't want to scrimp. Those photos are pretty darned good quality these days and have a lifetime warranty. So if it starts fading or gets scratched, I can have it swapped out. I included our OXOX (his daughter wanted that). I also included this line: "I can't wait to see you again, it's only a matter of time…" from the Broadway musical "Hamilton."

Jer and I loved "Hamilton" - It's special to us. But that particular line makes me burst into tears. It's at the very end of the play, Eliza singing to and missing her sweet Alexander. It just seemed appropriate.

In the top left corner, they've carved Jer's handwriting, taken from one of his many sticky notes. "I [heart] U" with the little smiley face he used to draw. I worried about adding that. I worried it wouldn't look right, that it wouldn't look like Jer's handwriting.

I placed the order and wrote the big ol' check in August and forgot about it for the most part; it would take a several of months.

AUGUST JOURNAL

Do you know it's your birthday tomorrow, wherever you are?

Are you going to celebrate atop the brightest star?

What happens to your big, beautiful soul tomorrow, anything?

I like the idea of your bright star being born again tomorrow. That it enters the world with fiery gusto ready to impact everyone it meets.

But having you as an infant doesn't do me any good. I wonder if you enter someone in the ER or maybe you already moved on - at least your essence - immediately through your tissue?

Do they celebrate you in heaven or are birthdays just an earthly pursuit?

Maybe they celebrate death days up there - the day you went to glorious heaven and joined the angels?

I wish you could come crashing back from heaven tomorrow, Aug. 6, in some form that could interact with me.

HAVE A GREAT DAY!

My parking spot was one of those 45-degree angle spots facing Pioneer Park - known locally as a park where some folks go to do whatever it is they do with drugs; buy, sell, shoot, snort, I'm not certain. I pulled in, sat for a moment watching the activity of the park - mostly sleeping - and sat with my phone.

This wasn't the ideal spot for this, but it was shady, I was between off-site work meetings and I needed to do it before the rest of my day unfolded.

I opened Facebook and began.

It was a post I dreaded, had given great thought to and I needed it to happen early-ish in the day before people began wondering why I didn't care about my husband on his birthday just because he died. I mean, just because he left the earth-plane. That's how my friend told me to phrase it. Left the earth-plane. Because he's still here, he's all around, he's always with me, so on and so forth. But that certainly doesn't help me as I sit in the shade of Pioneer Park.

The day before, I rooted through his box of keepsakes, old birthday cards, love notes, ticket stubs. And I found the birthday card I penned to him two years prior. It was still perfect. He was perfect. And in today's era of sharing everything on social media, I felt this inexplicable need to share that with anyone who would bother to stop and read it.

I talked into my phone, reciting the words in my head to use as my opener, then began reading my love note / birthday card. Every once in a while there was movement in the park - someone rolling over on the park bench then a conversation started happening. I was pulled from the tears ruining my blush to wondering if I'd have to roll up the windows and make a quick get-away.

Once everyone was sleeping again, I finished my post. I picked out some pictures that captured how handsome he was, how fun he was, how loving he was and hit 'share.' I watched the stirring in the park as this large piece of my heart scurried through the digital connections, landing in the palms and computer screens of anyone who might care.

Spot-checking my mascara, which hadn't budged, thank you waterproof, I opened the app a couple more times to see if anyone had liked what I offered the world today. How bizarre to put my heart on the line and sit to wait for approval.

I pulled out of my parking spot, and drove in silence wondering if this first birthday without him is worse because, in preparation, I kept telling myself how difficult it would be; trying to brace myself.

Oddly, I decided to run an errand and stopped at Costco to cash a redemption check. I looked at my weary face in the rearview, opened Facebook again - the likes were rolling in - and found my membership card.

Walking past people, lost in their own thoughts, I wondered if any of them would be surprised to know what this day means for me, to learn where I am in my day or that I'd just been crying.

I waited in line at the customer service counter, a rather long counter built to handle returns, questions, memberships and anything else a warehouse store utilizes to keep functioning, the fluorescent lights blazing overhead and hot dogs cooking in the deli.

"ERICA! ERICA" a man's voice shouted. I couldn't remember his name but recognized his face as a distant acquaintance. He was at the far side of the customer service counter from me. I waved politely but we did not move towards one another.

"YOU BEEN DOING ANYTHING FUN?" he shouted.

I offered a closed-mouth grimace that I hoped looked more like a smile, "No not too much."

Again we didn't move closer.

"I UNDERSTAND YOU HAD A DEATH IN THE FAMILY," he shouted as king-sized shopping carts rolled by, receipts being checked. "MY CONDOLENCES TO YOU AND YOURS!"

I gestured a wave to him with my $24 and turned to leave. He smiled and waved back "HEY HAVE A GREAT DAY!"

DOUBLE CAMP CHAIR

The weather called. I wanted to be out in that beautiful night air desperately but I didn't want to sit out there alone. I didn't know how to at first and I thought everyone would ask all sorts of questions. As I mentioned, no private outdoor space. If I want to sit outside, which I always do, I have to either go on the back porch and look into the windows of my neighbors, or sit in the driveway and hope no one passes by.

I didn't sit out for a while. Finally, I decided I did not want to be a prisoner in my own home so I bravely took my double camp chair, my journal and my wine and plopped myself outside in the driveway.

Mostly no one said anything. Perhaps they knew? I don't know. I don't have one of those neighborhoods where everyone knows each other. On the contrary. My neighbors are strangers except for the couple next door, the Russians across the street, our boozy-twosies couple and the family on the corner. I don't know anyone else.

So I sat outside. It eventually became more normal, I guess. The neighbor lady who sits alone in her driveway every night drinking wine. People smile and nod as they walk by with their dogs or toddlers, but no one stops to chat. They just leave me be.

If I'm feeling like creativity is calling, I've even taken my guitar out there to plunk out chords or work on a song. There's one older fellow who wanders by and asks for a concert each time much to the chagrin of his grown daughter trying to get him to move along, but otherwise, I'm just the neighbor lady who sits out there alone. In fact, most of these current neighbors likely don't remember me with Jer anyway. He and I only lived there one year together, our last year.

One night our Russian neighbor came outside to putz around with something. Jer used to yuk it up with him, telling him he wanted to try real Russian vodka with him. The Russian was delighted and told him absolutely! (I told him absolutely not).

The Russian wandered over and was a bit inquisitive. I finally asked him if he'd heard what happened. He said he hadn't heard but wondered why I sat out there alone. I told him a condensed version of the sad tale.

He responded with, "Ahhh well…. That's life."

Is it? Is that life?

At any rate, I pictured neighbors watching me out there every night, wondering about me but never speaking to me.

SONG:

There's a lady across the street

Who sits in her driveway and drinks all alone

In her double chair.

No one next to her, just the night air.

I watch and wonder about her
About that empty space that's beside her, is she lonely
Or just sitting alone
Missing someone or content with her phone?

She's out there most every season,
Holidays and weekends.
She sits alone and sips her coffee or her wine.
I wonder why I wonder who's on her mind.

Yea that lady's across the street
It looks tonight like she'd rest her feet in the lap
Of someone who sat there
Sat next to her in that double chair.
Sometimes that lady across the street
Will write or read as she drinks or plays guitar
Like she's just killing time
Killing time or distracting her mind.

She's out there most every season
Holidays and weekends.
She sits alone and sips her coffee or her wine.
I wonder why I wonder who's on her mind.

I'd like to ask her why she bought that chair, for two.
Do you think she wants to meet someone new?
Or is she missing someone she once knew?

174

SORRY ABOUT THAT

When he asked if I was married, I said no. That was the truth; I was not married. I also didn't see the point in standing there, shouting over the cheap, over-modulated country cover-band that my sweet, handsome husband, the love of my life, passed away tragically a scant six months prior and that I was standing here wearing a red cowgirl hat and red lipstick because the theme for the company fundraiser was 'western.' Not for any other reason.

He wouldn't have heard me anyway. The band was blaring and he was distracted.

"I like your neck," he said, and reached out, almost absentmindedly, to touch, my left elbow.

I didn't have to answer. The possibly-drunk-possibly-dense female acquaintance introducing at us chimed in "HER HUSBAND DIED, RECENTLY" she shouted to the table. Then she turned to me, "SORRY ABOUT THAT, BY THE WAY."

Sorry about that by the way.

There I stood in my stupid hat and lips, wearing a shirt I worried was a bit too low-cut for a work gathering, hearing this woman only loosely associated with the company, shout to strangers about the darkest moment of my life.

For a brief nanosecond my husband's handsome face and dazzling smile flashed through my mind. Touching my elbow again the man said "My wife died too, four years ago." I softened a bit thinking he saw me in that moment. "When we divorced!" Those who could hear guffawed at a volume far beyond what the joke warranted.

I smiled politely. "Well, I've been through that too and it's not the same...."

"Does Mike still work here?" barked the other fellow at the table, who apparently didn't care about divorce or death.

"Yes, he still works here."

"Tell him Dave says hello."

At least the woman apologized, I guess.

SECOND WEDDING ANNIVERSARY

The whir of the overhead projector, hooked up to a DELL laptop, competed with the blast of manufactured air-conditioning. I sat slumped in my small snippet of real estate at the conference table, toggling my attention between the presentation on paid versus earned media and noting how uncomplimentary the glare of overhead lighting is for every single person at that table; it emphasized frizzy hair texture, dark undereye circles (mostly mine) and bad skin. It also left me comparing the gloss versus matte finish of the many bald heads also seated around the table.

Though some of these faces were familiar, having crossed paths at other conferences, I wondered about them. I wondered what sad tales they might have to share. I wondered if any of them would care that two years ago today I wore a white dress, on the happiest day of my life. One year ago today I sipped gin and tonics with my sweetheart in a seaside hot tub in Cancun. Now I sit in a committee meeting and my man sleeps six feet underground.

I wondered if any of them remembered they contributed to a woe-is-her fund when they heard the news. I wondered if they looked at me and thought 'she's the one whose husband died' or if they whispered that to each other as I walked by them in the vast hallways. It felt like they did. I noticed their attempts at quick, clandestine glances at my ring finger so they could discern - most likely judge - what stage of grief I must be in and if I've 'moved on.'

I wasn't wearing my ring. I used to. It felt too bare and exposed to be without it. Then I began to feel uncomfortable as I noticed people, I'm sure unintentionally, checking my finger, seemingly at-ease when I still appeared dutifully committed. And I was. But I didn't like the check-ins and began to wonder what magical day I would wake up and declare 'THIS IS THE DAY I NO LONGER WEAR MY WEDDING RING!' Envisioning the litany of glances and questions that would have to be answered gave me anxiety.

I switched to just wearing the wedding band. I put the sparkler back in its box and the few times I've worn it since, it makes me sad; this constant little reminder of that one time I was completely happy. So I kept the band as that seemed to fit both with what was expected as well as what I was capable of.

But after a few months of that, I started to get anxious that people would ask me about my husband, what he did, how long we've been married - the usual. I wasn't ready to drop that bomb. I'm still not. So I switched my band to my right hand, leaving my left ring finger sadly bare and utterly exposed. No one has asked me why I quit wearing it but no one will ask me about what my husband does, either. That's a bit of a relief, for now.

I walked out of the meeting room to take a phone call. Debt collectors. "I'm looking for Jeramy Evans," the lady said. "I'm his wife." She confirmed his birth date, then said, "I'm calling on behalf of North Fulton Hospital," then something about an overdue account. I cut her off. "Well he died," I said. "His estate is in probate" (using the fancy words I'd learned). I hung up before she could answer.

Those are the moments of loss that are surreal; reminders, gut-punches of how life marches on while I'm stuck in an alternate reality. Today, on my second wedding anniversary, my mind is in Cancun while I fight my emotions in a deep-freeze convention center, fielding debt collectors calling on behalf of the place where he died.

What is happening? It's just the way this death-thing works, I decided. Daily little occurrences to make you feel like the butt of a joke. 'I GET IT! I'M THE PUNCHLINE!' I thought, almost out loud. I rubbed my naked ring finger and almost added "HAPPY ANNIVERSARY TO ME!'

That's the moment in a chick-flick where a random stranger would walk up with flowers and tell me I'm pretty or something. Then I'd tear up knowing it was my sweetheart communicating from the other side, knowing I needed that. Instead, I sit in this lobby noting how frizzy my own hair must've looked under those lights. And no one brings flowers.

I stepped out on the sidewalk amid the lunch rush trying to find patches of sunlight between buildings to thaw out. I noticed faces, men mostly, and found myself seeking kindness, familiarity, something or someone inherently masculine. I reach for my sunglasses knowing one minute into any type of exchange and I'd grow bored and restless.

Light rail swished by while I wondered how people move on after loss. How do people kiss or make-out again without feeling like they have to shower afterward? 'No matter' I thought as lines of people began spilling out of eateries. Today would have been my two year anniversary and I was roaming, pathetically, looking for the moment a stranger would hand me a flower.

Besides, if a man started talking to me, wouldn't the story of my husband who died come up and therefore end all conversation? It's like lugging around a very heavy suitcase with no wheels. No one wants to help you carry it. No one wants that burden. It's almost too much to bear. And while I know it's not my fault and all, I can't help but feel like damaged goods in some way. 'Here comes that woman with all that sadness.'

Just like my Uber driver the other day. 'Are you married?' 'No' 'What? You're so beautiful - no relationship?' I tell him, 'You know, it's the saddest story,' and I give him the super-condensed version. To which he responds by blinking his eyes a couple of times and returning to driving. He didn't even help me heft my actual suitcase out of the trunk. Too much baggage.

The conference trundled on at its steady, predictable pace; there is some comfort in consistency. Conference-goers gather in the hotel bar; a loud raucous affair, until it's time to wander to the ice breaker. Lanyards swinging, we all walked in succession to the evening event mostly wondering if there would be an open bar. There was.

As the night drew to a close, conference-goers mingled, finishing their drinks, while others said their goodbyes ready to trek back to the hotel. My friend and I stood at a high-top table. She was chatting with colleagues while I quietly hummed along with Bobby Darrin crooning 'Beyond the Sea,' through the speakers.

A distant acquaintance I'd met once or twice before was heading out and stopped for a quick hello. I'm not sure if he noticed my humming, but he took my hand and pulled me out to the middle of the walkway and began swing dancing with me. This was not a dancing event, there was no dance floor; just a plaza surrounded by tables. We were the only two dancing.

We danced through the song in stops and starts. I tried to lead, like I do, but he was sweet, his hands were warm and we laughed. When he'd spin me out for the turn and pull me back in, he'd cut out a beat - EXACTLY like my love used to do. Every time!

The night air felt cool against my skin as my mind wandered to dancing with Jeramy in the kitchen, trying to figure out that one beat. We'd playfully argue about which one of us got the rhythm wrong (it was him); who added or subtracted that one beat every time.

This guy did the exact same thing on the exact same beat.

I loved it. I didn't completely realize the gift at the time, because I was busy smiling, moving, laughing, feeling the music for that one song.

In the middle of the night, my eyes shot open realizing my love had paid me a visit on our anniversary, after all. And, knowing Jeramy, flowers would not have been enough. He gave me more. He gave me something I love, something I needed. He gave me warm hands, great music and laughter - he danced with me.

SEPTEMBER JOURNAL

If you could tell me one thing six months later, what would it be? I'm hearing you say that you're proud of me and you love me.

Back when we used to listen to ZBB all the time, that song Bittersweet, always got to me. It's one of the only death songs I've ever liked. I've always eschewed them, finding them too sad. But that one I love. I love his earnest delivery, I loved how grateful I felt to be singing along to someone else's loss while you sat by my side.

"It's Bittersweet, you see, you're not here but I can feel you

Every memory is on the tip of my tongue.

Close my eyes, see your face, hold on tight to yesterday

And when I wake it was just a dream.

It's bittersweet."

Now I obviously hear it differently. But the line that jumps out is when the dying spouse says "Go and live your life with no regret, don't forget how much I love you. - I love you...."

Go and live your life with no regret. I imagine that's what you'd want to say to me. I imagine you cheering me on up there, helping me get up for another day, helping me out of sketchy situations and leading me toward peace, light and brighter days.

THE FIREFIGHTER

He said he was going to teach me to play poker. A pack of cards appeared though I'm still unclear if he brought them as a pick-up ploy or if the bartender overheard and provided them.

"So what's your story you're not married?" he asked while shuffling a deck of cards as we sat at the bar.

"Not right now," I said. "I have been… twice. Umm…. One didn't work out but I have a lovely 10 year-old daughter. And the other, the love of my life, well, he… died… unexpectedly: pulmonary embolism."

"Oh wow…. How long ago?"

"March." It had been seven months.

He shuffled the cards and shook his head. "Yea there's nothing we can do about that," he was a firefighter and the shake of his head told me he'd seen that scenario before. "The only thing we can do is get them to the hospital."

"Right. Yea…. well…. No one did that."

He didn't say 'I'm sorry,' which I appreciated. He just shook his head with an inner knowledge that my story was a shame that likely didn't have to happen. I watched him shuffle poorly, "you need me to help you with that?" I joked. We'd already established that while I was a lousy poker student, I was a better shuffler than he; at least that's what he led me to believe.

He laughed, nudged me a bit and handed over the deck. I wowed him with my shuffle and reverse rainbow thing I'd picked up somewhere along the way. I realized there were plenty of seats available at the bar and he didn't have to ask if he could sit next to me. It began to occur to me he also didn't care how the food was.

"I'm Jared, by the way."

"I'm Erica, it's nice to meet you."

"Come here often?"

"Not at all, actually, I know one of the bartenders - we work together at her other job," I said motioning to Hannah. "How about you? I gather you don't since you asked about the food?"

"Not really. I'm a firefighter. But I'm a rover so I get scheduled at different stations. So I was driving by and thought I'd check this out. I didn't really want to go home so I thought why not. Now I'm glad I did," he said, smiling and gesturing toward me with his beer.

He was living in the basement of the home he owned with his wife; on the verge of divorce with three kids, 16, 13 and 10. "Shit I've got so much baggage, I'm sorry."

"Oh don't be sorry, please. Everyone does," I tried to sound casual but reassuring. Frankly I was so painfully aware of that truth, I almost teared up.

"K do you remember the hierarchy?" he said as he took the deck from me and dealt us each two cards. "Remember, game face."

I picked up my hand. "Game face," I repeated, peering at him over my cards, raising an eyebrow.

"Shit you can't do that. You can't do that eyebrow thing, that's cheating," he shook his head.

"What's cheating? What? Why?" I asked, laughing.

"That with the one eyebrow. That's so sexy - that's cheating."

I knew nothing about poker.

"Everything I know about poker I learned from Kenny Rogers," I told him when he asked if I was going to stay for the night's tournament - $5 buy-in. "I'm not playing in that."

"Stay, please? I want you to stay. I'll pay your buy-in and I'll teach you how to play," he was charming when he insisted.

"Do I get to sit by you?"

"Hell yes - why do you think I want you to stay? You'd better! Come on... it'll be fun."

I began to enjoy watching his hands; leaning close to him to see his cards as he explained them to me.

Hannah quietly refilled my glass when she noted what was happening and busied herself with other customers. There was laughter, there were side glances, a touch or two. I felt, for a few seconds here and there, like my old self.

"No, I said game face, not beautiful face," he said when we began our next hand.

"Aww.. that's sweet thank you."

"Oh stop it... sheesh," he said shaking his head at me. It was one of those 'you-hear-this-all-the-time-stop-acting-like-this-is-a-first.' I almost didn't know how to respond; I was so out of practice.

We played another round which I lost terribly.

"Have you learned nothing?" he joked. "You have to look at this like it's your wing -card. A two is a terrible wing card."

"But what about the Queen??" I laughed.

"A Queen and a two are NOT a good match. Let's try it again."

He took off his jacket, ordered another round and divvied up the cards. I liked him. He was fun. He looked good in his t-shirt, firefighter and all.

"I'm having fun, thank you. I hope this is okay?" he said.

"Why wouldn't it be?" I said. "Wine, handsome man teaching me how to play poker.. What's not to like?"

"Handsome?" he said with a bit of a boyish 'maybe she likes me tone.'

Before I could respond, he began rubbing at his chin "Oh I don't know about that, I'm not used to this," he said about the salt and pepper facial hair covering his jawline.

"What do you mean? I like it," I said and used the opportunity to reach out and feel its softness.

He explained he normally can't have facial hair for work but since he was off for a week or so he'd quit shaving. "I'm not used to myself like this."

But he wore it well. He had a nice smile and had those smile lines I love. People call them crows feet but I love them.

"K it's time to play - you ready?" He asked, taking my hand, leading me from the bar stool to the poker tables.

"I don't know if I'm ready. I don't know anything about it."

"You'll be fine, you've been practicing," he said showing those smile lines as he glanced over his shoulder. "I'll be right there."

He sat down, placed our drinks on the table and began. It was awful, the players were quite tense for a Wednesday $5 poker game. 'Why do they take it so seriously?" I leaned in and asked.

"You're doing fine, really. Don't worry about them, I'm right here," he said squeezing my knee.

The waitress brought my water but placed it on the far side of the firefighter. I reached across him, took a sip and set it down. He quickly moved it back to the far side.

"You know I did that on purpose," he said beaming.

"I figured," I said, reaching across his broad chest again. "Good thing I'm thirsty."

He shook his head, smiling, "You're something else," he said.

As per Kenny Rogers, we folded and walked away; both losing eventually but not before many whispers, playful touches and one or two good hands each.

"You want another drink?" he asked.

I hesitated, looking at my watch and checking in with the fizz in my head.

"Come on," he said. "One more. What else are you going to go do?"

I chuckled knowing he was right. Hannah caught my eye and gave me a subtle thumbs up with a question in her eye. I nodded yes.

Firefighter bought me another glass of wine and we sat where we could hear each other talk. We talked about his job, the weightiness of if. We talked of other nonsense that goes with being an adult, having kids, divorces and husbands that have died.

He was everything that makes me nervous in a man - die hard risk-taker. Everything about him. From his Harley, to his job, to his hobby of off-roading in Moab.

We closed the tab and stepped out into the crisp night. He showed me his motorcycle - red; my favorite. "Will you ride with me?"

"Never" I said.

"What? Why not?"

"Those things scare me. Besides, I can't take the risk. Not until my daughter is grown. You've got 10 more years until I get on that thing. But it's beautiful."

"Can I walk you to your car?"

"I was hoping you would." I linked my arm through his and we wandered under the parking lot lights.

"Tonight was such a surprise, I loved it," he said.

"Yes thank you - a pleasant surprise."

He stepped closer and wrapped me in his firefighter arms in a tight hug. A few times.

"I really want to kiss you but I'm not going to because I'm a gentleman," he said as he pulled away from our hug, shoving his hands into his pockets.

I was mixed - most of me would have liked to be kissed, I think. But most of me was also glad for the get-out-of-kiss-free card. Which, should be noted, was highly unlike me; the old me, at least. I loved a good kiss. Hell I even loved the bad ones. I loved that moment he finally decided to take charge and move in. I loved noting where his hands went, how his lips felt against mine, what his facial hair did.

But tonight I may have been glad. I wasn't sure. Part of me wanted him to. Part of me was hoping he would; wondering if he would. Part of me didn't know if I'd know what to do if he did.

I climbed in my car, watching him walk toward his bike. I took a breath and tears began streaming down my face. Resting my finger near my eyes as if trying to push tears back in, I picked up the phone and it was 11:33 p.m. - Jer's magical number. My clear sign from Jer. He was there. He sent me an 11:33.

I cried most of the way home. I just wasn't sure how to feel. It was the first of anything, really, since Jer passed away and I wasn't sure what to make of it. I didn't know how this would all go. Is it possible to enjoy someone's company without thinking of him? To want to be kissed, admittedly wishing it was Jer, but wanting it anyway? Was he there? Was he watching? Did he care? Was he disappointed? Was he glad someone was putting a smile on my face?

The dual confusion of having enjoyed the evening and 'what about Jer' lingered for days.

I thought of the firefighter. I thought of Jer. I thought of that surprise evening and how it conjured up a genuine smile or two.

I didn't have answers for any of it, but felt grateful to have felt something beyond sorrow and grief or faking my mood. I might have even felt like my old self for just a moment.

TIME CURRENCY

Time is a fickle beast, isn't it? While we understand there are 60 seconds in a minute, 60 minutes in an hour, making up the 24 hours before the clock resets itself, the passage of that time... that is a different story.

Time flies, time stands still, time is fleeting, it's exact. Time is money, it waits for no one, we lose track of it, we relish it when it's free, it's valuable yet we waste it.

The tricky part: In the currency of time, the units we're all living and exchanging, are different. My $5 (five minutes) is not the same as yours.

There's a quote by Albert Einstein, "Put your hand on a hot stove for a minute, and it seems like an hour. Sit with a pretty girl for an hour and it seems like a minute. That's relativity." You see? That's also the difference in time currency.

You run into an old friend after not seeing her for a few years and her infant is now a three year-old running her ragged. Your concept of those three years - magically creating a toddler where an infant once slept - is not the same unit for your worn-out, weary friend who's anxious to get the kid potty-trained, finally, and into kindergarten.

You've just exchanged different units of time; you're using different currency. Sometimes it feels like an international market place where everyone is wandering around with different forms of currency - dollars, euros, soles etc.

A week is a flash while on vacation, but an eternity for an out-of-work job applicant who was told a decision would be made soon - different units of time.

We do it all the time. It's the coworker who waltzes in late with a cup from Starbucks. You've just exchanged different currency for the 15 minutes you spent sitting through your budget meeting.

This is important because time currency gets meaningful when we well-intentioned mortals start to pass judgment on how someone else is spending their currency. Whether it's a death we're talking about, a divorce, a career change, anything.

"Boy she got over that fast."

"Wow he's already dating."

"She didn't last long at that job."

"They're already living together."

Naturally, it works in the opposite direction too:

"She should be over that by now."

"Gads it happened a year ago."

"Hasn't he moved on yet?"

"How can she still be working on that degree?"

Time currency is the reason we need to offer grace to one another as our unit of time is not the same as anyone else's.

When I stood at the mouth of this grief tunnel, I was in awe - in the truest sense - of people who had gone through it before; people who were farther along the path. 'How did they ever do it?' How could someone possibly exist in this tunnel for two years?!?!

It was beyond comprehension.

Likewise, when I hear or read of someone sharing their story; talking about loss and how far they've come - and it's only been a few months - my eyes pop out. As someone farther along the path, it's difficult to comprehend their sense of making it through the tunnel when so little time has passed from my broader perspective. And, I would wager there is someone five or ten years through the tunnel wondering what I think I'm talking about.

You see where I'm going here - those are different units of time. The me who wrote about the firefighter is using a different time currency than the me sitting here today, sipping tea and visiting her through pages of pen scratches.

I have to remind myself of that when I start thinking *How could I have thought seven months was a long time?! Why would I have written or even thought that then?!* (yes, judging myself).

That currency of time, those lonely nights, the coming to terms with a new quiet, is a very, very different currency.

I remember the slog. I remember the endurance test. I remember Saturdays, which used to be filled with love, laughter and fun, but now it was just me on the couch, staring out the window watching the shadows grow up the neighbor's house. Tick... tock... tick... tock...

I remember walking in from the garage and dreading when the garage door stopped its closing grind as the quiet stillness in the house was deafening and that moment is when I heard it loudest. Tick... Tock....

Those nights you don't want this day to continue anymore, but you don't want to go to bed because it's empty and cold and his space looks so cavernous, so you just sit, stuck. Tick... tock...

It's the realization that when people start chirping on about

'It's Friday!' 'yay it's the weekend' 'do you have any plans?,' your thought process is 'yay…..here are 60 hours I get to fill by myself!' You want to scream "NO I DON'T HAVE ANY PLANS, MY HUSBAND DIED!!!!' instead you say 'oh not much, just keepin' it low key,' and they skip out of work early.

It's having a house so quiet you hear the tick, tock

It's staring at your sweetheart's photo just knowing he'll wink, or speak or something.

It's actually *feeling* the… time…. pass….

THAT is a unit of time currency that is almost indescribably different from any other unit that people exchange and society is clipping along at a much busier pace, there is no way they could understand.

Seven months in 2018, was an eternity.

During one Saturday endurance test, I wrote this song:

Time moves differently when you're trying to kill it.

Time just hangs in the air, its own heavy spirit.

Father Time ticks on the wall, and the fridge it hums

But that sun stays put, tomorrow doesn't seem to come.

So I'll pour me another drink and watch the shadows fall.

All the thoughts I could ever think, amount to nothing at all.

Time moves differently when you're trying to kill it.

When you're not having fun, you're just trying to will it…

To tomorrow or last week or a year from now

Just push through this moment doesn't matter how
It's too much time on your hands, than should ever be allowed.

So I'll pour me another drink and watch the shadows fall.
All the thoughts I could ever think, amount to nothing at all.
Time moves differently when you're trying to kill it.
Well bang, bang, tick tock... another minute down.

WHISKEY

I lifted the highball glass to my lips taking in a small sip; a very small sip. I've always believed whiskey to be a sipping beverage and never understood the many people who gulp down a throat-full and wince, gasp and pull faces at the burn. They're wasting the very best part.

I let that sip sit in my mouth for a brief second, before letting it slide down my throat. I sat still in that moment and closed my eyes, feeling its journey. I took in a large breath, the whiskey spread into my lungs, its heat filling my chest.

Whiskey takes me back to him; to nights at his place. One sip, less than a thimble-full, transports me. Every time.

There are certainly more ladylike drinks to choose, and not to worry, I often choose those too. But whiskey... whiskey is full of fire, heat and history.

I ring his doorbell and suck in my belly in case he can see me from somewhere. I always get a little rush of butterflies as soon as I hit the doorbell. I know I have seconds before he'll be standing here. I wonder why I don't pause a second longer to make sure I don't have lipstick on my teeth or to fluff my hair more.

His footsteps grow louder and I clutch the bottle in the brown paper bag with a bit of hesitation. I try to find a pose that is sexy casual, casually sexy - some stance that looks like something a bit better than I am.

The door flies open and he stands, backlit from the house lights, beaming; arms outstretched inviting me not only to step forward into his home but into his whole world.

He wraps me up in a hug, kisses my cheek then pulls back to tell me how happy he is that I am here, rubbing his hands up and down my arms to warm me up.

As he moves for my hand to lead me into the house he notes the brown bag.

"Ahhh… what's in here?" his mischievous eyes darting from the bag back to mine.

"Oh, a little something I told you'd we'd try," I say just a tick nervously.

Whiskey can be so divisive and many people have already formed opinions. *What if he hates it? What if I just dropped $40 on a damn bottle of whiskey he will never drink? Can I take the bottle home? Is that in poor taste? Would a man know?*

He takes the bottle, slides it out of its paper bag wrap and studies the label "Ooh whiskey huh?"

As I begin my excuse song-and-dance (a skill I've honed from my mother) 'we don't have to,' 'don't feel pressured,' 'you may not even like it,' 'it was just a thought,' he was already pulling wine glasses out of the cupboard.

"Okay, how do we do this?"

He clearly hasn't heard any of the many 'outs' I've provided him and if he did, he's choosing not to acknowledge a one of them. I love him for that.

"Well, we start by putting the wine glasses back in the cupboard and using something more like...." I walk by him trying to brush him nonchalantly, "... more like this." I find a glass similar to a highball glass. I purposely grab one, so we could share, and pour a shot.

"That's it?" he says.

"Yea, it's got more alcohol than beer and wine so you just don't need as much."

He throws the whole shot back in his throat, does that familiar head-shake/ wipe-this-from-my-tongue-now kind of face that people pull when they chug whiskey. I think he even stuck out his tongue through all of this.

I laugh.

"You're not supposed to do it that way!" I squeal, still watching his facial gyrations. I knew he disliked whiskey and now I knew why. He drank it like everybody else - Fast, furiously and with the hopes of forgetting. He must've thought he'd like this better just because I'd bought a better bottle than he was used to.

"I've always done it that way," he says once he comes to.

We laugh as I pour another shot. I suck a small drop from my thumb and glance into his deep green eyes - deep like an olive green of sorts; an old soul's eyes disguised behind a boyishly handsome lens.

"Like this," I say and I take the glass to my lips. "Small sip. Very small - like so small you'll think you won't be able to taste it."

He watches closely as I take my sip, closing my eyes, tipping my chin up and feeling the whiskey slide. I take a breath.... and then... there it is. That heat; that glorious heat fills my lungs. I never speak or get distracted during this first sip. I just close my eyes and take in the moment.

"That's how you do it," I say, handing the glass back to him.

His eyes search my face, his playful smile showing his eagerness for more.

"It's all about the heat," I continue. "It's about quieting everything just enough, to feel it go down. Then when you think it's right at about your lungs, inhale, you'll feel it - boom - spread through your chest."

He doesn't entirely believe me and I think he feels a bit silly but he does it my way anyway. He takes in a small sip, and waits for the right moment to inhale. "Wow! Man!" he says pounding at the heat he was feeling in his chest.

"Then if you wait a minute, you'll start to taste all those bottom notes; the deeper flavors."

I don't tell him I am a novice myself and that I don't really *know* anything about whiskey, this is just how I like to drink it.

I catch his eye and he leans in for a kiss.

I guess he doesn't care.

I took the last small sip and looked into the empty glass. I pictured drinking whiskey out of that shared highball glass and out of wine glasses. Then I pictured whiskey in red solo cups at BBQs, our flask at the party in the park and out of the paper hotel cups.

For a brief second I considered pouring another but for what? I set the glass down and leaned back, feeling the heat linger and mingle with my memories. When both began to fade, I got up and poured just another sip more.

MY OWN TIME CAPSULE

It was the first time I thought 'man, I can't really read this.' I was lying on my stomach in bed, trying to focus my aging eyes on my journal and writing - it was just too close. I got out of bed and went searching for Jer's reading glasses. We'd gotten to where we'd chuckle at the font size on his phone as it could not be adjusted any larger and his arm couldn't stretch any farther when trying to read.

I slipped on the glasses and sort of felt silly. My smirk turned into a bit of a giggle, in spite of myself. I just sort of laid there giggling. It was one of those genuine moments of turning to share it - share the chuckle - and remembering he's gone. Then feeling foolish because him being gone is what created this moment in the first place. But there I sat, giggling - feeling a bit funny in Jer's readers and giggling that they worked.

Then I cried a bit. I had this terrible realization that THAT'S what life is - a shared experience. Someone to share those moments with. Someone to chronicle your life, keep track, pay attention to you and your moments as you slip into your senior years. I had just lost the witness to my life. And even though this moment was not a wedding, or a baby being born or something more significant, it seemed like a moment couples move through together - wearing readers for the first time - to commiserate and tease a bit. That night it was just.... me.

I decided to take a picture of it. Even though it was not me smiling on a beachside vista somewhere, I decided to take a selfie. There I am, in bed, weary, having slogged through another day, wearing-readers-for-the-first-time selfie.

From that point, I decided that the witness to my life would have to be me and that I'd snap photos of not just the happy moments but the real and raw moments too. I decided my camera roll could also serve as my time capsule and as a reminder, a chronicle, of the moments when I was low, really low. I took selfies at the cemetery, selfies on the floor propped up against the wall after crying. I took photos of my various journaling spots, I used the camera's timer to capture solo hikes and other solo accomplishments.

Of course, the photo roll has happy moments too. But quiet moments alone tell a bigger story. I'm sure there's a modern day lesson in there about comparing your whole life to someone else's highlight reel.

The year before all of this, I made a personalized family calendar as a Christmas gift for Jer and the girls. The calendar was for 2017 but the photos were from everything we were doing in 2016 at that time. Silly photos, trips, weekenders, driveway time - just a time capsule, really of 'last year at this time.'

These personalized calendar programs and platforms are amazing and allow you to add as many photos as you'd like. I didn't know at the time what a hit that calendar would be; how much we would all love it; how often we'd all flip through just for the photos.

That became my new job - calendar maker. The girls would eagerly ask if I was going to make another one; they wondered what photos would be selected. Anytime I'd hint that I might not make one, they gasped and started pleading.

So I made another one for 2018 using all of the memorable moments from 2017 and it was hung on the wall in the kitchen.

By the time March 1 came and went, that calendar took on a whole new meaning. It served as a daily reminder of how good life used to be. Things we used to do, fun we used to have, a life that used to be good.

The calendar became interesting because for at least the whole first year after trauma, the brain goes into 'last year at this time' or 'we should be _____- fill in the blank.' It's constantly comparing the now to the then. *Constantly.* So the calendar didn't help. Month after month, there was Jer's smiling face. There was my own smiling face that I no longer recognized. I didn't recognize the woman in the photos - so light and breezy; smiling and crazy-happy. Who was that? I would stand and look at the photos and try to remember what it was like to be her, to be them.

Like seeing a long-lost photo of yourself and you marvel at how young you and everyone else look - a moment of proof that you were once young and that you have, in fact, aged. I wanted to crawl into those pictures and warn her - warn that woman. Tell her not to get too comfortable in that life. Tell her what was to come. Then I would think better of it and decide to let her have that moment.

As we got closer to autumn, Victoria asked again if I would be making another calendar. I was surprised as surely there was nothing in 2018 worth putting in a calendar. It was a dark, abysmal year full of nothing but sorrow and sadness. But I didn't want to add to that sadness by not doing the calendar, so I got to work on it.

There were two months - January and February. There was the Family Award night that Victoria created (Jer won for 'wasting time on others' - ha!). There was Jer's Daddy Daughter dance with his youngest daughter for Valentine's Day. There was a mimosa morning in there too. And there was a selfie of us - our last one - in the hot tub in February; we got a wild-hair to sneak into the hot tub at our old apartment (we knew the tricks to get in). It was a kid-free Saturday, winter, yes, but sunny and bright.

Then it was March. I've always thought funerals were a bizarre thing to take photos of. I hadn't developed my philosophy on photos serving as a time capsule yet and I wouldn't have had the wherewithal to take any in the first place. I guess I wish I had some. I wish I had a photo of all the flowers in the room, all the people lined up out the door to the street. I wish someone had snapped a photo of me bravely standing next to my husband's casket greeting guests, in my most vulnerable moment.

I had a few sent to me by other people: the bright, sunny day; the group shot of the siblings; the girls and I touching the casket one last time. That's about all I had - but who wants that on the kitchen wall? I opted for a collage of selfies with Jer.

I rifled through the photos on my phone, trying to fill a calendar in a year that was full of such sorrow. I knew I couldn't put big black squares from March to December and I knew Victoria needed the calendar; she likes tradition, she loves the photos, she loves turning to the new month.

Slowly the calendar came together. Perhaps I sit here today and wonder if it was therapeutic, even. The practice of going through moments and seeing the faces that are around you lifting you up. Willing to accept you in your sadness but serve to buoy you up - lunches, concerts, arts festivals, wine nights. I realized there were moments of genuine smiles and laughter. I did have parts and bits that I enjoyed - as much as I would have with Jer? Certainly not. But I still enjoyed them.

I also used my solo pics. I put in the pics of me at the cemetery and the pics of me crying. I added the selfie of me wearing Jer's readers. It was a calendar of moments and those were some of my moments. I was concerned Victoria might react to those or ask questions (she always asks questions) but she didn't. It was almost as if on a cellular level she understood why they were there and perhaps liked it - perhaps it reflected how she was feeling inside too.

NOV. 4

My phone chirped a reminder and I glanced to catch it before the screen faded. "Anniversary."

The screen went black; I just stared at its empty face. November 4. Today was November 4.

"I'm sorry what?" I said to the colleague standing in my office. They didn't seem to notice my distraction at least, if they did, they didn't mention it.

Oh my goodness what have I done? Surely he doesn't mean that. Surely he doesn't mean he is on his way here - to my work - with a churro. Damn. How will I pull this off? How will I explain this to anyone who might ask? I decide he is likely just kidding and try to busy myself with work.

My phone buzzes. It's him saying he's here. *Crap he really came. He really did it.*

I begin the 10 minute walk to get from my marketing/PR office to the front entrance of the Zoo. 10 minutes to wonder what's about to happen. I've only seen the guy once, at Costco, and have been fine with just being Facebook friends. That's all it's been all this time.

We are not dear friends. We are not 'drop into each other's work' friends. I barely know his name for crying out loud. And yet, here I am, walking by the gorillas on my way to the entrance. *'What if he's not even cute?'*

I get to the entrance and see him through the gate. He's pretty cute.

In the middle of a Tuesday afternoon, there he is in gym clothes - *okay so this guy's unemployed.* He has not one, but two churros - one for me, one for my daughter. *Smooth.*

We sit on the edge of the fountain out front chatting, briefly, only 15 minutes maybe. Against all my better judgment, I like the guy. He is funny and bold with a large energetic presence that I like.

I was wrong about him being unemployed. He started his new job the day before as a manager at Wendy's and currently has Tuesdays off. He's on his way to play racquetball, hence the gym clothes.

Our brief conversation gets cut short by my boss pulling up to the front entrance catching me completely off guard.

"I gotta go, that's my boss"

"Yea I need to head to the gym anyway," he says.

With that, we go our separate ways. I walk back to the office with two churros in my hand and a smile on my face. Huh! How about that - he's cute and I liked him. I had no idea if he liked me or if we would see each other again.

Then he texts - "I'll always remember this week cause I started a new job Nov. 3 and got to see and talk to you on Nov. 4."

On the next November 4, a year later, I get a call from the guest services office that someone is here to see me. I wander down to the front with a spring in my step wondering what my sweetheart has up his sleeves.

I get to the entrance and there he is, beaming at me in the rain. He had arranged to leave work, went home and changed into gym clothes, to recreate our first real interaction. He brought me two churros. We hugged and kissed in the rainy afternoon.

I'm both surprised and not at all surprised that he has remembered this day. I go back to my office and enter it into my phone so I won't be caught off guard again.

I was caught off guard by the notification. I didn't have the heart to delete it and I liked the reminder anyway. I wish the alert would happen at a time I could truly get lost in thought, but I like pausing for one second - pretending I'm about to walk to the front of the zoo, wondering if the Costco guy is actually cute.

THERE ARE NO WORDS

One brisk Sunday morning in December, Victoria and I bundled up and went to the cemetery for a visit. We like to go sit, eat donuts or some other bribe; I never want visiting Jer to feel like a sad punishment to her. We started walking up and I could see half of Jer's face poking out from under the recent snow-turned-ice that covered the ground.

I immediately began jogging through the snow to his face, letting out guttural sobs of some sort. Frankly, I still don't know what sound was coming out of my face (I wish I could demonstrate for you). His headstone was in and no one had told me; no one warned me.

Rather frantically, I fell to the ground and tried to clear the headstone of the ice with my bare hands and it just wouldn't budge. I couldn't see it. Was it accurate? Did it look okay? Was it what I wanted? Was it like the Photoshop rendering? I kept making that weird sound, my nails breaking but the ice wouldn't move.

I ran back to the car and got my ice scraper to use as tool for prying the ice. Careful around his face, the ice began to crack and lift and there it was. For a brief second I thought it said "I CAN wait to see you again, it's only a matter of time." I was frantic again to brush all snow and ice from the headstone to clear it.

Victoria watched her mother making those sounds, ripping her nails off, brushing away the ice and sobbing. She understands the moment but I wonder what her memories are. I always envision her writing a memoir some day and trying to put some of these moments to words.

I cleared all the snow and the ice and brushed out all the grooves (turns out windshield scrapers are good multi-use tools). And there he was - my guy, my Jer, on a granite slab, set for life. I took pictures, I chatted with Victoria about it, trying to normalize the moment; make my earlier reactions less traumatizing for her.

I was struck by what an exhausting learning process death is.

Back to what I learned. Lesson three - Don't get caught off guard.

Please tell your funeral workers that you'd like some notice when your person's headstone is installed and perhaps they normally do and I was an oversight, but I'd make a specific note.

I couldn't wait to go back - by myself with my journal. I needed time to process this latest step and to see what it felt like to sit with him there. I just felt I'd been robbed a moment. Had the workers told me the headstone was in, I'd have gone out at a time I could have properly processed how impactful and permanent the headstone felt. I needed that time and instead, I was trying to put on a brave face for Victoria, trying to be less awash in utter grief - just partially awash. It just wasn't the moment I envisioned.

Lesson Four: Don't text pictures of the headstone to anyone who isn't prepared.

I owe Jer's family an apology. I did not mean to catch them off guard. I did not mean to catch them unawares. I just... I wanted to share that the headstone was in (they had been asking about it) and that I thought it turned out great.

But you see, that moment I had when I saw half of Jer's face sticking out from beneath the ice, that's what I did to them via text. I just sent the pics of their son/brother in granite - no warning, no heads-up, just BOOM! And people need to be prepared for that. Their reaction, if I received any at all, was very muted and not at all what I was expecting - just flat "wow... there are no words" or "it looks great."

I love his headstone. I love his face looking at me when I visit. I love the meaning behind each line. And, selfishly, I'm glad I didn't ask anyone for an opinion because, from what I can tell, I'm usually the only one who visits him out there. Which, if I'm being honest, is how I like it.

UNEXPECTED
GOODBYES

The wine glass slipped off the counter top and into the sink. I'm still not sure how - was I holding it? Did it slide on water? I gasped and hoped it was thick enough glass to survive the drop. It wasn't; it didn't. It shattered all over the stainless steel. I just stared.

I was so sad. Just..... sad. I sort of cried and sort of bellowed "Nooooooooooo!" I wanted to punch something and I wanted to go to bed. I was just so sad.

I have much fancier glasses but I'd go out and hurl all of those into the street to have this one back. I love my fancier wine glasses but this set was Jeramy's and, man, did we have some great moments and conversations with these glasses in our hands.

This set was more manageable, we could throw them into the dishwasher, they weren't so tipsy. We loved this set. I'm sure they're just from Target or Walmart, I know - they're totally replaceable. And yet they're not.

We used to have four. We broke one, then another. We were

down to two before Jeramy died. Each night since, I'd reach for one and say to myself 'man I hope these never break.' 'Man I'll be sad if these break.'

Then it did. Right in front of me and there was nothing I could do to stop it. There was no saving it. While the moment is vague, I do remember thinking I was being careless, this didn't have to happen.

I'm still sad. I type this tonight, with a bit of dark chocolate and wine in the last of our glasses. And yes, I'm careful. And yes I'm already sad that it might break.

There are goodbyes we decide - like 'today is the day I'll get rid of his socks. I feel ready and able to do that.' Then there are goodbyes we don't decide. That we aren't ready for. That we don't see coming.

Just like the wine glass.

Like deleting Jeramy as my emergency contact on the various forms that crop up (typically while a receptionist or nurse stands waiting).

Like having to change forms from 'married' to 'widowed,' (that word).

Just like each utility company that needs to remove his name from the bill.

Like the arm of his readers that broke off in my hand.

Like the wine glass paintings we did that crashed to the ground when the hook gave out.

Just like my red coffee pot. When the time came to move out of my folks after my divorce (meeting Jeramy helped me make that decision rather quickly) I was buying a few items for the house. He came over and laughed when he saw the ridiculous, itty-bitty 4-cup coffee maker I bought. I figured it was just me, it would do.

The next time he came over, he brought a brand new adult-sized coffee pot, 12-cups. "Big enough for two," he winked. It was red, my favorite. My sweetheart got me a red coffee maker. He opened up the box, quickly glanced over the instructions and got out his label maker. He printed out an 'OXOX' and slapped it on the bottom.

I loved everything about it - the color, the coffee (the amount), the gesture. That Mr. Coffee brewed happily for us for years. And it brewed with comfort for me after Jer.

Then one day it stopped. It just wouldn't brew. I tried and tried knowing for sure the next day it would brew again. I just refused to believe I'd have to get rid of Mr. Red - my gift from Jer.

I denied it. I stupidly bought coffee for weeks - weeks - unable to handle the thought of getting rid of Mr. Red. *"I wasn't prepared for the fact that I would slowly lose more and more elements of our time together,"* I journaled.

I finally thought Jer might actually want me to buy a new maker so I wasn't wasting money. I bought a new red coffee maker and left it sitting in the box for another several weeks, unable to say goodbye. My 'ol Mr. Red sat on the counter, the new imposter sat in its box and I spent $4 a day buying coffee at the shop up the street.

It was finally time. I don't remember why I decided that day was the day. I pulled the new red coffee pot out of its box and tossed the instructions. I peeled off the 'OXOX' and placed it on Mr. Red II and right then, the clock read, 11:33 a.m. I smiled, 'he approves.'

I took old Mr. Red, that brewed so many cups of joy, and placed him next to the garbage can, underneath the Merry and Bright sign that still sits above the door. He looked sad. This wasn't a goodbye I chose.

When the time came to ready tomorrow's coffee. I washed the pot, ran an empty brew and hit set. Right as I did, the clock read 11:33 p.m. Jer had blessed it. Twice.

COSTCO BEACH

The lady checking my Costco receipt took it from my hand, glanced over it, into my cart and back over the receipt. "You're going to love that shirt" she exclaimed, gesturing to her own body. She was wearing the very shirt that was sitting in my cart. That's not quite what I pictured when this soft, blue, slim, slouchy shirt pulled me in.

For some reason, I envisioned sexily wearing this shirt, near a fireplace, sipping wine with… with someone. A man. But I'm not sure who. As I thanked her, she told me she owned them in two colors and I pushed my way into the parking lot.

◆ ◆ ◆

He has something up his sleeve, he always does. We have spent the past five months or so seeing one another and frankly, since our date on New Year's Eve, we've been virtually inseparable. But I still get nervous - good nervous. Anxious, giddy, combustible excitement. He is unpredictable and electric that way.

He happily chomps his gum, not revealing where we were going. He has an indistinguishable spark that floods even the most mundane tasks. Every last one of life's moments are heightened. We have a date tonight but based on the spark on his face, something unique is about to happen.

Assuming we are running an errand, I grow curious watching Jeramy veer through the far reaches of Costco's vast parking; past several available parking spots, beyond the cart drop-offs, beyond the gas station area, out to the outer edges.

"Ha! What are we doing?"

"You'll see" he says with all the enthusiasm of a boy ready to show you the critter he's captured in the yard. He parks Betts, rests his elbow on the center console and reaches out for me, wrapping his hand behind my neck pulling me in for a few quick but meaningful kisses.

He hops out of the car, pops the trunk and pulls out a blue tarp. With one giant swoosh, the tarp fills with air, and rests on the ground. Next, a red Coleman cooler.

Here we are in the Costco parking lot on a weeknight. I look around a tick nervous. The warehouse store is open. Granted we were off in the corner, but still... people are around.

He reaches into Bett's trunk and pulls out two beach chairs, opens them up and wrestles a blanket out of the back seat.

Am I supposed to sit down? Are we spending time here in this parking lot? Is this the surprise? The temps in SLC in April can either be glorious or sketchy at best. This particular April evening, the temps are rather chilly - obviously he is aware, hence the blanket.

I'm horrified. He wants me to sit down in the Costco parking lot, during business hours, in the cold and do what? I don't know what to do or what to say. A pallet driver passes by. I feel anxious. I know the driver is going to say 'what are you doing?' or 'You can't be here.' But when he drives by, Jer waves at him and shouts 'what's up man?' The man smiles and waves back, almost knowingly, and drives by. I mean... the tarp! The beach chairs! He said nothing??

Jer gestures to the beach chair as though offering me my throne. He's beaming. Taking my hand, he leads me gently to my chair and puts the blanket over my lap. I smile and say nothing other than something like 'wow… well thank you.'

Remarkably, Jeramy is unflinching. No hesitation. No 'gee, maybe this wasn't such a good idea..'. He is unabashed and unapologetic.

5300 South is a major rush-hour thoroughfare, everyone trudging home from work, and here I sit; perched in a beach chair on a blue tarp in the Costco parking lot while my date roots through the red cooler.

He pulls out glasses. GLASS glasses, straws, ice, gin and diet tonic. He even packed limes, a knife and a cutting board. He puts himself to brisk work slicing limes wedges, and making a perfect gin and tonic. He hands me my favorite drink and says "you've been missing the sun, the warmth and wanting a beach. And I can't afford to take you there this year, so I thought I'd make one for you!"

Spring was late, we were overdue for warmth and here, this man, creates a beach for me - complete with a blue tarp to signify the ocean - in the parking lot of where we met, Costco.

Lifting the G&T to my lips, I take in a drink. He leans over, kisses me beautifully and pulls out a card.

April 22, 2015

Mi Dulce Hermosa Donette,

It was two years ago today that I reached out to you in a simple Facebook message to let you know that I did indeed flirt with you at Costco. Therefore, I think it is appropriate that we celebrate such a simple yet powerful demonstration of character I exhibited after I felt the desire to do so, in the place where 'this' (us and our relationship) all began. Also, since I am known to some as "Costco" I should probably go there more often to relive the simple yet profound meaning this place has become....

...So on this the 2 year anniversary of the day I reached out to you on Facebook, I want you to know that I love you. And not only do I love you but I feel a humongous amount of hope for everything that "this" has to offer us, our children, our families and frankly all of those around us.

I wish us well on our journey together and know that if it is anything like the past 6 months then it is going to nothing short of AWESOME!

Love Your darling hunky, and handsome, Jer

His sentiment is beyond lovely and unlike anything anyone has ever said to me before. We both tear up. He kisses me again, making sure I'm still warm. I suddenly don't care. I don't care that we are in the parking lot (thanks partly to the gin) I don't care that people can see our crazy-in-loveness, I just don't care.

The warmth was too far away this year so he brought it to me. He hears me. He listens. He cares. I matter. He made it happen. Just as he always does.

Leaving our beach behind, he leads me to the Costco deli, to treat me to dinner - we choose pizza. Jer pushes me beyond my comfort zone - he is overt, he is public, he is bold. I'm giggling that we're leaving this random beach setting in the parking lot unattended. But he doesn't mind.

We sit in the chairs, on the blue tarp, listening to the traffic, pretending the passing cars are ocean waves, eating our pizza, madly in love and completely oblivious that people are around, hauling groceries and trying to get home. We are sitting on a beach and all because I said I needed/wanted it. That's Jer. That's his attention to detail and his willingness to put forth effort.

I lifted the tailgate, put my sweatshirt, the one the receipt-lady was wearing, in the back of the car, along with the toilet paper and winter boots.

I grabbed an errant shopping cart floating in the parking lot as I took my own back to the cart drop off - the one we drove past that day. I glanced up toward that area, toward that spot of the parking lot, I pictured a blue tarp. I pictured a cold spring evening.

The waiting Subaru had apparently grown impatient and honked at me. I waved apologetically and hurried to return the cart.

NOT-SO-HAPPY NEW YEAR

The end of 2018 was not-so-quickly approaching. Facebook started doing its thing of generating a grand highlight reel to share with you so you could show off what a great year you had. Mine was cobbled together from the few neat moments I had, but that's only because those were the moments I shared.

I sat with that for a second and thought 'those aren't my highlights. Facebook doesn't get to decide what my highlights are.'

I found my favorite pics from 2018 and posted the following:

Facebook Dec 28, 2018 -

"I'm not going to share Facebook's look back at my 2018. Yes, I was able to travel to Hawaii and Alaska to visit my wonderful family. I was able to meet a walrus, hold a toad and forge some new and meaningful friendships. But those were not my highlights.

My highlights for 2018 were much simpler than that. Two months of sipping coffee on weekends (and maybe a mimosa or two), one last musical, one last gathering with friends and one last soak in a hot tub on one of those glorious mid-February days full of sunshine and hope that spring just might make an appearance (our last selfie). I'm so grateful for that time.

As you're with your family this holiday, take photos of the mundane. Take pics of the everyday moments happening right in front of you. Take video. Capture voices and movement.

I am profoundly grateful for your love and support. Life takes a village and I'm learning that more each day. Love you all!"

While I couldn't crawl out from under the weight of 2018 fast enough, I was grateful I once heard in grief group that clicking over to a new year - one where your person didn't exist - could be tricky.

I worked the cold ZooLights shift that night and got home to an empty house in time to take a tear-stained selfie at 11:33 p.m.. I don't remember if I managed to see the new year.

There was a meme that went around at the time (I think they do every year) that says "Hey, 2018? Bye Bitch!" I wished I could have given it more than one 'heart.'

I spent New Year's morning alone, getting tipsy on mimosas, playing guitar and journaling my hopes for the new year.

"My sweetest, I decided to make an occasion out of New Year's Day anyway. I decided life is about occasions and moments and sometimes they create themselves (birthdays and holidays) and sometimes, we make them - moments of laughter, moments of joy. So I've decided I'm going to make a damn occasion out of this on my own. You and I would have been having mimosas together. We would have toasted the time together.

This is New Year's Day dammit, and I'm going to welcome it the way you would want me to. The way we would have done. With joy, hope and a sense of occasion. That's how we lived, you and me. I'll never regret that."

I hung up the new calendar and made another drink.

2X4

I continued to dabble in song writing and had written several, but I was still only singing in private, on the couch while playing guitar. I figured that might be good enough for me for the rest of my life. I envisioned telling people some day 'Oh I don't perform anymore that was a long time ago.'

Apparently, that wasn't good enough for Jer who began to get bold in his opinion on the topic. One day, in January, I woke up to a text asking if I'd sing the National Anthem at an expo. It was a weird offer, from a number I didn't know, the timing was odd, they asked for me by name it just made me pause 'huh… singing the National Anthem is easier than singing a whole show.' Weird.

I went downstairs to make breakfast and Jeramy's phone buzzed. I still had his phone and I was still paying for its service; just hadn't gotten around to shutting it down. Obviously it never buzzed these days and most times it wasn't even charged. This particular morning is was charged and it buzzed right while I was standing over it. I looked at the phone and it said 'You have a new memory.' It was a picture from February 5 that came through at 7:33 - It was a memory of the two of us when I sang at the gala for the Utah Shakespeare Festival in 2017.

So on January 31, his phone sent a reminder about Feb. 5 and it happened to be a pic of me all dolled up to sing with Jer suited up in support.

"Huh…. that's weird," I thought.

Jer didn't stop there. That very same day I got a call at lunchtime from the Heber Valley Cowboy Poetry and Music Festival. We had done our Patsy tribute up there in the past and I was scheduled to sing there the year Jer died, which of course I canceled. But that day, as I sat in the car on a beautiful, sunshiny-winters' day, they were asking me back in October to sing, they wanted to know if I was ready. "We'll give you two shows - Patsy and whatever else you'd like to do."

Patsy Cline, I'd be reuniting with Patsy Cline. I felt a bit sheepish about it after my big dramatic breakup and all; I wondered if she'd be open to a reconciliation. I wondered how I'd feel nine months from now, in October.

Later that same day, my girlfriend who was heading up her own non-profit fundraising gala asked if I'd sing at her event as well.

It was as if Jer decided 'today is the day,' then pummeled me with messages about singing all day. I'd always told him, 'I need you to be loud and clear,' and he was. Not only was the message loud and clear, he set it up for me so each singing event could build on top of the others - a National Anthem, background music at a couple of events, then a full show in the fall. It almost felt like permission to find myself again.

I took it all as a sign. Hesitantly, and boldly for my state of mind, I said yes to all three.

ANOTHER MOUNTAIN

A bit of angsty anxiety seeped in as the first death-iversary crept closer. You know the date is important, you know you've accomplished something, you know it has weighty significance. When you lose someone you love suddenly (and I imagine the same is true after illness) it permanently etches all of the surrounding events and moments in time, into your mind, forever. Those days, perhaps weeks, leading up to the death, are an excruciatingly vivid memory. And since your mind has such a firm hold, you mentally binge-watch your own 'end of day' over and over as the year-mark creeps closer. You just relive all your lasts - last time I spoke with him, last time we kissed, last thing I said, last thing he said, last thing texted.

Even if you keep your mind on track for the most part, the air smells the same as when... the daylight looks the same as when.... The in-store decorations are the same as when... It's all an ominous, eerie, not-very-subtle reminder.

The march toward that first finish line looms big through this whole marathon. What to do? What will you do? How will you mark it?

Every person is different. Some folks don't want to be to around so they leave town for the anniversary every year, needing a distraction. For me, I feel the need to be contemplative. I want to do something nice for myself, and take time to sit and reflect, just think about Jer, our last few days, how we didn't get to say goodbye, how I've persevered since his passing. I like to spend some time thinking about that brave woman who drove through the dark in the middle of the night to Atlanta. I've never felt like I'd enjoy boozing by a beach somewhere on March 1 anyway. It's a special, commemorative day for me and I feel like its owed its due. But again, that's a personal decision for everyone.

March 1 of 2019 was a mostly sunny day. I took the day off and I used the day to spend time with myself. I went to the cemetery twice, once in the morning and later that day and treated myself to a massage. I bought my favorite lunch, and just spent time thinking and reflecting. It was a relief in many ways to have the day finally come and go - It just released some tension.

From my journal entry:

"I think back to one year ago at this time, driving blindly to Atlanta, wondering what on earth was happening to my idyllic life.

I cry for that woman and I'm so impressed with her - persevering, continuing to see beauty, to look for small moments of joy. She did the remarkable.

That woman who drove to Atlanta was courageous and has character. I admire her. She also has added depth and a greater understanding of the human experience.

That woman does not have the answers to any of it, but she got up and showed up. She was productive at work, she maintained the car she loves. That woman even found ways to stay connected, see friends. She took trips, she saw Alaska she smiled genuinely, she made new friends too. That women poured herself into Victoria - continued to show up for her, do Christmas, ice skating etc while shielding her from sadness as much as possible.

That woman poured her heartbreak and woe into writing. She poured her extra time and sorrow into learning guitar.

She did all this while being utterly heartbroken."

I guess I was proud. I was proud that my photos from the year were me still trying to participate in life. I tried. I may not have been my most witty self, but I tried.

"I guess that's the dichotomy of this whole process. Being happy enough that others are not uncomfortable, showing enough sorrow so they know you're still grieving. Being public enough so the world is aware of the struggle, but private enough that I can grieve fully. Having enough fun so life still seems worth living but not so much it feels disloyal. Showing enough sorrow to Victoria so she understand the magnitude of the loss, but shielding her from the depths."

Marking the first year is a monumental accomplishment. But what people don't tell you is after reaching the summit of your first mountain of a year, you turn around, thinking the work is done, and you're staring right at another mountain - year 2. No one tells you that part. Wait, what? But I just did all that!

The second year was worse for me. People are slightly less concerned about you because "a whole year has gone by," a little more is expected of you in work and life because "a whole year has gone by," and you're no longer numb but still quite raw. Like having a sensitive tooth and going to the dentist - just that raw spot in your heart that's going to get jabbed and poked at any moment.

FINDING MY VOICE

Journal 4/26/19

I sang publicly for the first time since you left me. It was a low-pressure gig, an annual gala, and we were background music.

I bought a new dress. I wore false lashes and sparkly jewels.

The band guys were fun, the atmosphere was fun and I sang. It felt good hun. I enjoy the music - the songs. I love watching the musicians at work. I love seeing people enjoy the music too.

I guess I enjoyed it. I guess I went from thinking I'd never sing again - ever - to standing up there tonight.

I hope they were pleased - I was. I laughed and had fun and I felt the music in my body.

I'm grateful - I'm grateful for friends who helped gently pull me back up on stage and in front of a mic. I'm grateful for the opportunity to sing in a low-pressure setting to let me see how it feels. I'm grateful for these amazing musicians who back me up and support me.

I'm so grateful for music.

With an anthem and one performance under my belt, I focused fully on my upcoming performance at the cowboy festival.

Heber, UT is a beautiful valley nestled over the mountain near Park City, about 45 minutes east of Salt Lake.

At the time, the Cowboy Poetry Festival had been going on over 25 years. They brought in talent and fans from around the country, all passionate about country/western music and lifestyle. The booths out front sold everything from custom-made cowboys hats, handmade horse saddles, jewelry and bolo ties to fur coats, western paintings and Navajo flat bread. The Festival featured music and poetry all weekend long beginning at 10 a.m. each day. Those people take country music very seriously.

I performed there once before, doing a tribute to Patsy Cline. When Heber called me on that sunny January day requesting Patsy, I wondered - Would she be there for me? It's not hyperbole to say I feel, deep down, that I need her on board with me singing her music or she won't be there with me and I need her to be.

So I bravely agreed to Patsy that day, which I'd need to dust off, and I also went to work researching, writing, creating - a tribute show to the other women of country music. This is a show I'd been contemplating for a while, mostly because I wanted an excuse to sing their music - Dolly, Reba, Tammy, Emmylou, Loretta and more. I smile now just thinking about it.

This task, the job of preparing a show, focusing on material and lyrics became a good focus of my time and effort. It gave me something to do, so when I was home alone for extended periods of time, I had a project. I had something I was working toward and that was supremely helpful for me. (I also had moments of dabbling in writing that would eventually turn into this book). It was creative, it was engaging and I hoped it would be rewarding.

I also decided at this point I had learned enough guitar to strum along with a few songs. Remember, country music can be rather easy, 'a few chords and the truth,' the famous adage goes. With my band hooked up to the amps, I felt confident I could memorize the chord progressions in a few songs and strum along while the band did the heavy lifting. This would give the look and feel of some of those country greats plus I would get to play my guitar on stage.

The planning process took me to St. George, Utah, to visit a friend who is also a costumer to see if we could figure out something for me to wear. St. George is about a 4 ½ hour drive south of SLC and it proudly flaunts the gorgeous red rocks that make Southern Utah a destination.

We decided to peruse the vintage shops. St. George has a hefty retiree population and sometimes retirees (and the clearing out of estates) can offer some pretty special dresses. We found a beautiful, vintage teal and silver dress, straight from the '60s - perfect representation of Patsy and the cocktail dresses she wore and it actually fit. Well, it fit well enough to sing in for an hour.

We continued to thumb through the vintage racks and I saw the corner of a red sequined shoulder pad poking out through the other garments. I wasn't sure what that shoulder pad belonged to but I knew that was my Women Of Country dress. I grabbed hold of the shoulder pad, and found it belonged to the most fabulous long-sleeved sequined dress, hit just above the knee, with a high collar and a sweetheart cut-out, a là Reba / Dolly, straight 'outta the '80s. It couldn't have been more perfect. And, in all the glory of 1980s sequined fabric, full of all that stretch - it was great fit! We added some sparkly, silver trim and I was good to go.

I loved the get-away. I loved the visit and I loved the dresses we found.

JER'S TIME CAPSULE

As the slog through year two continued, I busied myself with my shows and Victoria's various activities. Month by month, we flipped the family calendar and studied the pictures.

There's the selfie I took with the stack of Jer's work shirts, the day I donated them. There are many of me at the cemetery in all types of weather. There is the pic of me on my solo hike before I got nervous about mountain lions. There is a teary car selfie on the rainy afternoon I went to the cemetery to pick out Jer's headstone. There's me in my cowgirl hat at the work fundraiser. Me with my pals at the work conference where I spent my second wedding anniversary.

I began to realize that I'd rather be me today, than me last year at this time. Looking at the calendar in 2018 was a very painful reminder of what I'd lost and I yearned to crawl into those photos. But now, in 2019, I stood there, looking at all the shots of me navigating the worst year of my life and thinking 'man I'm glad that's not where I am. It's better to be me today than me last year at this time.'

Pics of me smiling with friends but remembering how I was itching to be home with my journal; pics of me leaning against the bedroom wall with a runny nose and smudged mascara on those nights I couldn't even make it into bed; the pic of me lying in bed alone wearing Jer's readers. It ended up being the most beautifully complex patchwork quilt of a time capsule.

I still make calendars. I have added making one for my mom to my to-do list - with ALL the family - (it's a very time-intensive project so proceed with caution). And, as I write this, I'm working on the calendar that will hang in our kitchen for next year.

One of the things I've grown to love about creating the calendars, is replacing last year's pics with this year's, noting growth and change. And each month, I still fill one of the little boxes with Jeramy's handsome face; I like to see him on my wall all year long. That's when my second realization came. Every picture of Jeramy has already been taken. There are no new pics. There will be no new pics.

His time capsule is complete.

MY ROBIN

Each morning as I head into work, I typically leave a rambling Vox for my sister, or sisters, depending on the news of the day. Voxer is our favorite messaging app which works similar to if a walkie-talkie and an answering machine had a baby: You just push the button and talk, leaving your message, gabbing until you fill your 15 minute quota then start over if there's more to say (you'd be surprised how often there is). The message waits until the other person has time to listen.

I love it and keep in touch with a lot of people that way. It's easier than trying to match up timing for a phone call, allows for great storytelling and also offers great companionship. I love opening the app, seeing I have a lengthy message from my sis or Matty while I start my walks, for example.

Anyway, that morning I was rambling about who-knows-what and gave my sister quite a start when I squealed out "arhhhhhhhh - sheesh! Sorry bird suicide," and went on with my story. In our subsequent back and forth she wondered what the hell I was talking about.

I told her it happens all the time - all the time. I'm driving along and some bird flies from out of nowhere and sprints (is that what birds call it? buzzes?) in front of my moving car.

Sometimes it's close but I know I'm not going to hit it. Other times it's so close I worry I'll have a mess to clean up.

Bird fly-bys happen all the time. I assumed they happened to everyone but she said it never happens to her. After our chat, I began to really pay attention to bird encounters. I started keeping track. I reported back and sis was blown away by the regularity of the happenings, as was I.

There's just a strange phenomenon with birds and me and I have to confess - they're not my favorite animal. They make me a tick nervous.

Once, when Victoria was little, we visited her grandparents and went to Rooster Cogburn's Ostrich Farm in Tucson, Arizona. One of the attractions there is a large netted space were you can go in and feed lorikeets - beautifully colored, small parrots.

I unwittingly walked in the netted area, took the lid of my nectar and out of nowhere, all these birds swarmed around me, landed on me, dug their little feet into my bare arms. I squealed! I tossed the nectar, flailed my arms and ran out of there. I couldn't help it. I'm just not super comfortable around them. I prefer them over there and I'll stay over here, even though I don't like how that makes me sound.

So, this non-bird-lover began to take more notice in birds and began doing a bit of research. Once I started finding pages on the spiritual meaning of birds, bird sightings and their presence - I became fascinated.

Bird fly-bys were happening to me all the time and I began to notice birds were visiting me at the cemetery, often. And I don't just mean the angry swarms of Canada geese who strut around like they own the place, pooping on headstones and fussing about who should fly out front. I've journaled noticing one lone bird circling high overhead. I've journaled about the songbird, perched in the nearby tree, that sings to me while I sit.

One night, on my walk, I noticed a bird who seemed to be noticing me. He'd been flying around and finally sat on a fence a ways in front of me. He watched me while acting like he wasn't. We both kept our eyes on each other. I got closer knowing for sure he'd fly away, but he stayed. Closer... closer... this bird stayed. I wondered if he was brave enough to sit there while I passed in front of him. I think we were both getting nervous. Closer... closer...

The second I got to where he was, he took off with a start, doing a fly-by right in front of my face! I shrieked and flinched, luckily didn't make contact with him in my flailing. That bird flew off, circled overhead as I laughed, out loud, at that moment of excitement and surprise - like a game. It felt like the bird and I just played a game that ended up with me being the winner - laughing out loud and smiling.

I journaled, *"I'd been feeling so blue tonight and I couldn't help but think/feel that was your way of cheering me up; making me laugh; making me smile. It worked."*

Then there's my robin.

Lone driveway time felt daunting and lonely and very exposed for a very long time. Eventually, I got used to plopping on the right side of my chair, with my laptop, journal, phone and sometimes guitar on the left side; wine or coffee sitting next to me on the ground.

I began to notice, each morning, a robin would come to visit me. He typically sat on the eaves of the Russian neighbor's home, directly across the street. He would sing for me in the morning or sing along as I played, just keeping me company. He's pretty much there every morning and I miss him if he's not.

But it wasn't until I sat outside one evening that I really began to pay attention. I was working on a song, sitting there trying to pick out chords on the guitar. It was a song about trusting your heart to love again, written from Jer's perspective - or from the perspective of the person who's gone.

"Please trust your heart to love again

and know it's okay that you do.

I know you'll love me always

But I know your heart....

There's room for him too."

My robin appeared but this time he was on the ground with me. He landed not far from where I was sitting. He'd hop and look at me and sit. I tried to just hold still so he'd stay longer. I've never had a bird intentionally get so close to me, to trust me that much. He just hung out for a while. We both seemed very content to have one another there for a time.

I was reminded of a story Jer told me about a robin he began seeing shortly after his grandmother died. He noticed the robin had a small black spot on its heart; a rogue black feather maybe. He saw that particular bird often, appearing outside of his window, sitting on the fence.

Back to Google - after that night's encounter I began to get curious about robins. Their presence has a lot of significance. Robins are seen as messengers of heaven; the old adage says "When a robin appears a loved one is near."

They symbolize new hope - that even after the darkest winter, there is hope for spring. A 'sign from heaven encouraging us to move forward with determination.'

Interesting.

Birds. Who'd have thought?

I am chagrined to consider the Medium was right - that I'd have a strange attraction to birds - and them to me - but perhaps it's true. I notice them in ways and at moments that I never did before.

These types of encounters are difficult to explain and difficult to get other people to understand. I've learned to become very selective who I share unique encounters with as I can't bear to have them explained away. "Well yea robins are everywhere this time of year," "Robins always sing in the morning," "Well I see robins every day too," so on and so forth. People can't help it - apparently everyone is a bird enthusiast, knowing all about migratory patterns during the various times of year. I don't like the doubt it creates in my mind when I know had an encounter with an energy beyond my driveway, beyond my double camp chair.

So I keep these moments to myself. I have a few trusted souls I share with and of course, my journal. I love keeping track of anything energetically different, especially in nature.

Maybe it is just migration patterns. But doesn't navigating this life become much more interesting if you believe... even a little?

THE TUNNEL

My boss, in trying to explain what we were all feeling after his round of layoffs (I was spared) said "it's like the five stages of grief."

I just bristled. I sat there behind my COVID-19 mask with my lips pursed and bile building up in my throat.

"Where are you on that spectrum?" he asked.

My first thought, none of your damn business. My response "I'm fine."

Fine. What is it about that word? Such a catch-all word. It must verbally be something like the junk counter in my kitchen - hand towel, chargers, half-empty hand sanitizer, lunch bag that didn't get emptied out yesterday, half bottle of wine, a few bills. It's just this place of all this stuff we don't want to bother with right now so it seems to gather there.

That's kinda what 'fine' is like - this catch-all word we use when we don't want to be bothered to deal with the question being asked. It's polite enough so as not to offend, but it's used often enough in other settings that there is this underlying, unspoken thread of a conversational dead end.

He went on, "See some of you may still be feeling anger, some of you may still be feeling denial, and I'm at acceptance because - "

"I'm familiar with the stages and I'm fine," I spoke plainly. I wasn't. We never really are when we use that word, are we?

I'm painfully familiar with the infamous five stages of grief - written for people going through terminal illness of their own, not for those grieving the loss of a loved one. It's referred to so often it leads many to believe it's a linear climb up a staircase and once you reach the top, acceptance, everything will be fine, right? For a time I wondered if this should be a book on why the five stages is a misnomer and not helpful as it has given us all this strange belief that we're stepping up a staircase of sadness and each step is a better, brighter step than the day before.

Naturally it's the book one reaches for when they or someone they love is standing at the beginning of the deep, dark pathway of grief. Picture Ichabod Crane in *The Legend of Sleepy Hollow*, looking down the two paths in the forest on his way home desperately trying to avoid the Headless Horseman - one path slightly brighter with more light coming in, the other enshrouded with crippled trees and no light; just shadows, darkness and despair.

That's grief. The rest of the world gets to skip down that other pathway and you have to forge ahead down the dark, shadowy trail - mostly alone.

I have a journal entry from March 7, 2020, barely over two years from Jer's passing, in which I explain it like a cave or tunnel. I've actually used this analogy for friends going through divorce, loss of a parent and such.

"I envision standing at the opening, looking down its throat. Others get to go up and around it but you, you have to go through it. They can peek in on you through little mesh peep holes as they walk on top; make sure you're okay. But you have to go through it. Step by

step. Through the darkness - with little moments of light each time someone opens a hatch to check on you. But slowly, steadily, you move through the tunnel.

You can't speed it up, you can't shorten it, you can't go around it. You just have to get through the tunnel.

Slowly, you begin noticing bigger spots of mesh which allow for more light. Eventually, the tunnel is all mesh. You're still in the tunnel because you're still different. But light and air reach you more easily. Then you notice flowers and vines can cover the metal.

It's still a tunnel, a new path, something forever different about you. But it takes on its own beauty - flowers grown from your fertile soil of struggle, sweat, tears and sheer will."

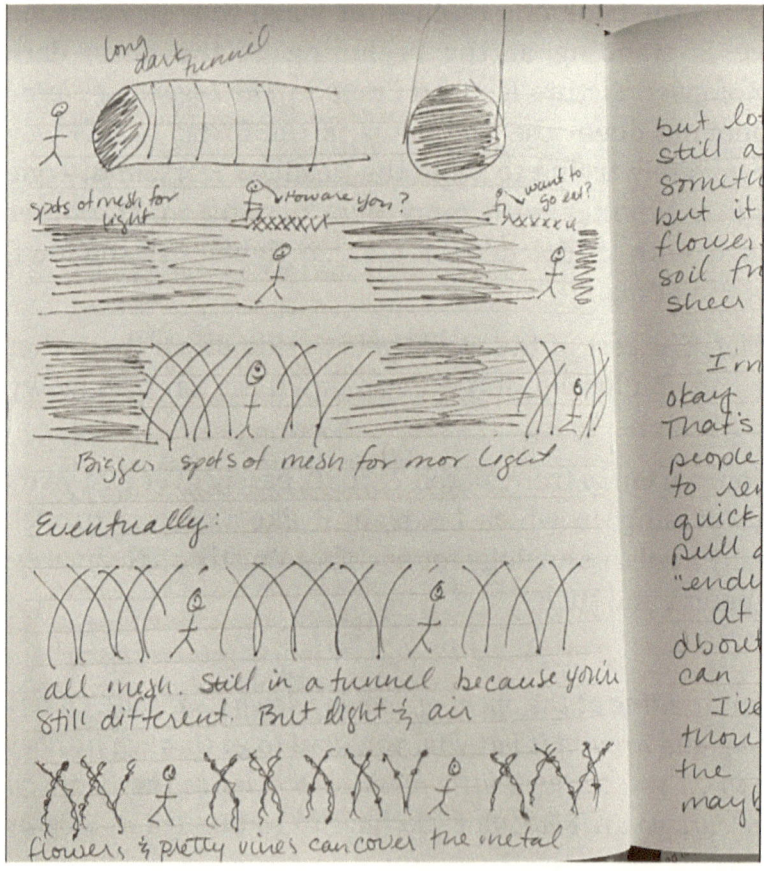

Grief is not a staircase - maybe something like the stair climber at the gym perhaps in which you never reach the top because the stairs keep coming. Ooh, maybe it's like the staircases in the old musicals that Fred Astaire used to dance on up and down, up and down, up and down.

There's one more piece to the five stages theory or puzzle - acceptance. I've decided that's the wrong word. One never really accepts it; makes it sound like you're okay with what happened and of course we're not. We never really are.

But I do think we surrender to it.

I think we surrender to this new state as it's too crushing and exhausting to do otherwise. Actually, now that I think about it, I may have had that backward too. Perhaps we don't surrender to the awful thing that happened to us. I wonder.... Do we surrender to the notion that it's going to be okay? Or that maybe we're going to be okay?

I was having those thoughts as I was nearing the end of year two. To mark Jer's passing, I typically take Prosecco out to my mom and dad's, we toast to Jer, we toast to making it through another year. I make a chocolate cake - Jer's favorite (which he ate from a bowl filled with milk).

That year, my sis brought me a large glass vase filled with daffodil bulbs. She said she got them because she thought they were the cheeriest little flowers in yellow (Jer's favorite color). They're the first flowers to bloom in the spring as a sign that the worst is over. She felt they were symbolic of my life - that I'm through the worst of it. That maybe I'm through the long, dark winter of my life and perhaps at the beginning of my spring.

I liked that gesture; I loved that thought. I liked that I was realizing I didn't want to be 'sad' all the time. (COVID was right around the corner at this point - Ha that would teach me).

One night at our grief group we talked about when it's okay to be okay. I pondered that for quite some time, still do, in fact. As I've walked down this path, any time a person told me that I'm 'going to be okay' or that I'm 'healing' - yes they do it often - I bristled. I was quick to point out that I'm actually not okay. I'd pull a face or tell them I'm 'enduring.'

The fellow widow (ugh, that word) in grief group told a story of bumping into an old acquaintance she'd known years ago. This person asked (genuinely) 'How are you doing?" My friend responded, "….. I'm okay. I'm okay!" And, she actually *was* okay. She meant it. She was bright and lively telling this story that she said she was okay and she meant it, she felt it. She was about seven or eight years into her tunnel.

I had a girlfriend at one point say 'You just have to decide what your identity is, what it's going to be and when you no longer want to be the grieving widow.' I was taken aback and to be fair, at that point, it was likely way too early in my journey to hear that.

But I've not forgotten it.

When is it okay to say you're okay? It's scary because it communicates a strange 'you don't have to worry about me anymore' to the world. Obviously there is comfort in knowing people care about you and that they're there to support and help, but does that change at some point back to just a friendship? Or a relationship that is less about making sure you're getting up in the morning and sleeping at night and more about grabbing a bite and a movie?

I stopped telling people "I'm enduring" as I decided that's full of negativity and, frankly, aren't we all enduring something? I switched back to "I'm fine," "I'm well," "I'm pretty good."

I think we round a bend, not to acceptance, but to surrender. We can surrender to the notion that - and this is putting life's most complex and painful moment simply - our person is gone, but the freight train of life is charging forward and the world is a better place if we decide to hop on and start living again or, more importantly, *our* world is a better place if we decide to start living again.

Perhaps there comes a time when you have to consciously decide to unwrap from the heaviness of constant sorrow and slip into something a little more comfortable.

"I've been sitting with the notion that I'm okay and maybe it's okay to be okay. That I don't have to be sad. That I can eternally miss Jer, but still find reasons to smile, still find joy. Perhaps both can exist at the same time. And, perhaps, it's okay to let people know I'm okay. Is that okay?

I don't want to declare the war is over, but the battles are less frequent

So I'm okay, but I'm not.

It's fine, but it's not.

I'm sad, but I'm not.

I'm happy, but I'm not.

I'm lonely, but I'm not.

I'm alone, but I'm not.

I question, but I don't

I accept it, but I don't.

I surrender."

MS. PATSY CLINE

"Let me find the dark places - the places where I've hid music; where it doesn't belong. Let me bring music back to the foreground of my soul and my spirit - not as something that took you away, but as something to help me heal. Please let performing and music help me heal."

I loaded my two vintage dresses and sparkly shoes in the car and headed up to Heber for the Cowboy Festival. I'd been working on the material all summer, and journaling about stepping onto that stage again.

Since the cowboy festival runs through the weekend, and my shows are on two different days and two different stages, we typically stay in Heber overnight to avoid having to drive up and down that canyon. Plus, soundcheck is often bright and early in the morning.

Autumn in Heber is stunning and this October, Heber really put on its own show; sunny with glorious bursts of fall color dotted throughout the mountain valley. Sweet Matty came to town to help with the zippers, buckles and laughter. His calming presence and humor kept the mood light, allowing me to focus.

The Women of Country Music show was first and played in the larger auditorium. I remembered most of the words, I remembered most of my stories, the band played mostly spot-on, it was mostly perfection. I was pleased.

Afterward the audience said such nice things, they wanted photos, they all seemed thrilled. So was I and it was a relief to have one show behind me. Afterward, Matty and I went and grabbed a bite and, since I still had the Patsy show to get through the next day, I needed to keep things low key and rest my voice.

Our Tribute to Patsy Cline was the next morning on the Campfire stage, a more intimate venue that seats only about 100 people. They're packed in there pretty tight and the show was sold out.

We did our soundcheck at 10 a.m. and already had people lined up, standing in line with their coffee, waiting to get the best seats. People trekked from all over for the show... Colorado, even as far as Nebraska. One man said he bought tickets as soon as he saw me on the schedule.

I went backstage to finish getting ready, they let everybody in. The band took the stage and there we were. The microphone, the music, Patsy and me.

They didn't turn off the house lights. It must've been an oversight; it was a bit distracting at first. Almost too much information. Too much detail of the audience. Also, sometimes people mouthing along don't always know the words and your brain can end up following along.

But then I realized, with the house lights up, it allowed me to see the faces, the smiles, the eyes closed in reverie, the head boppin', the whispering to a partner about a treasured memory. I ended up being grateful for all that information.

They were riveted. They were as big of Patsy fans as I was and we all got to share an amazing hour together.

I journaled *"I love Patsy. I love Patsy's music. It feels so familiar. It feels like worn jeans, a fuzzy blanket or a loving hand to hold. It just feels like an old friend. I've had times, and did on Saturday, where it felt like it's Patsy signing - as though she's paying me a visit. Truly. I wonder if she wheels and deals with God and He gives her a hall pass to come sing her songs again. It feels that effortless. Easy."*

A man came up after, who had actually seen Patsy in concert back in the day, and said "I'd like to say great show but that wasn't you up there, that was Patsy. Patsy paid us a visit." He said I so perfectly captured her that it had to have been her.

That afternoon, as Matty and I were leaving Heber on our way back to the Salt Lake valley, we stopped into a Wendy's to grab lunch. Wendy's will always make me think of Jer, but as we sat there eating, my ear caught a familiar chorus. As I listened more closely it was our song, the song he sang to me when I assumed he didn't know what he was singing, "Come to Me," by the Goo Goo Dolls. It's a song I never heard before Jer sang it and I never really hear it anywhere and there it was- In Wendy's, as I sat there in bright red lipstick and false eyelashes eating french fries.

"...Come to me my sweetest friend

And this is where we'll start again..."

He was there after all. He'd been there the whole time.

NEW FRIEND

You know how on the first day of school you ask your kid, 'did you make any new friends?' Sometimes they do and it's based on age 'she's seven and I'm seven.' Then they get older and it's more to do with where they sit in class or maybe a shared chuckle learning soccer in gym.

Had my own mom asked me that yesterday I would've been able to say, 'yes, I made a new friend - her husband died and my husband died.'

My how the years change us.

Janet reached out to me through my work email having connected the dots of my Jer being the same Jer she and her husband went to Lake Powell with years ago - before my time.

Her husband died in an accident six weeks prior and she was looking for some kind of advice, wisdom, ideas for dealing with grief. Said she'd been thinking about me a lot over the years and couldn't help but reach out.

We both agreed our husbands were likely in cahoots up there and we were both glad for it. I told her, "I'm no expert, but I can tell you what my path has been like and I can tell you what's been helpful for me."

Huh. How about that. I used to be standing at the beginning of that tunnel, now I'm looking back at someone else standing in the mouth. I'm still in my own tunnel, can I also check on her too? It's a strange sort of duty, I feel, to try to be of service in any way I can. In my bleakest hour hearing that I would "breathe again" was a mantra I held on to for months, years even. I needed those words at that exact moment and now I'm sharing them with someone else. "I can tell you you will breathe again. You will even smile again and it will feel genuine, but it takes time."

She talked about her six weeks as though it were six years and I had to remind myself how differently time moves when you're living in such a surreal existence (VR goggles). My weary heart having been in the tunnel longer, knows that six weeks isn't even enough to be considered the tip of the iceberg.

This friendship has turned into monthly dinners and check-ins. I'm grateful for it. I'm honored to be an escort through the tunnel. It's been helpful to her to hear what my journey was like; what was helpful for me and so on. I warned her about year two just like someone warned me about New Year's Eve and how hard it was to click over to a new year in which your person never existed. I was prepared. So was she, when her year-mark passed and she turned and faced her second mountain.

Our friendship has been helpful for me too. It's given me a chance to go 'hey…. Hey I'm doing okay.' Or 'Hey that used to really bother me but I've learned to live with it, or work around it or the pain is different.' It has allowed me to pause and realize the silence isn't as deafening as it used to be. The free time is still vast but not as dark and heavy. The bed is still large but I almost can't remember what it's like to sleep next to him so it's also comfortable.

Early on, when I would tell my mom stories about other widows (ugh) she pretty much always responded with "maybe you two could be friends." I hated it. I hated the implication that all women who've lost a spouse should and could be friends. I

246

envisioned accumulating a 'gaggle of grievers,' I'd call it - what a fun party that would be.

But maybe mom was right after all. There is something uniquely special and valuable in this type of friendship. It's like a one-on-one grief group with new insight, perspective and hope.

THREE YEARS

Today marks three years since the passing of my sweet Jeramy. He has now officially been gone as long as I knew him. We dated roughly a year and a half, and were married about a year and a half.

I recently heard a thought that resonated with me: To think of that time as an era. My Jeramy Era. I like how that reframes things in my brain. It feels like not only was that time a gift, something to be celebrated, it also leaves a shred of hope for me afterward - What is next? What's the next era? What chapter will I put in my book next? It feels like there is more for me and that's helpful and hopeful.

I guess, I don't feel him around as much as I used to - do I? Maybe that's because I'm not as desperate for a sign? Eager for one, always. But not desperate. Perhaps the constant searching lifts - Not because I don't deeply want a sign but because the brain knows it's a bit futile maybe? It surrenders. I surrender.

I say that knowing full well that my third year was a tumultuous one for the world - with COVID and quarantine and life as we know it being upended. Perhaps I had larger distractions? Or one could argue I didn't have any distractions as there was nowhere to go, nothing to do and no one to do it with. Just isolation. Was that helpful? Jer would have been the *best* quarantine partner, by the way, we never would have wanted it to end.

When I was in Georgia, unable to get out of bed, reading in a Facebook message that I would "breathe again," I did not think it possible - not at all. When I got back to Salt Lake, and after the funeral, that FB messenger and I met for dinner to compare stories - she was two years into her tunnel and I was two weeks. She talked about the season of grieving being over; that it lifts. Naturally at two weeks in I didn't believe her and thought she was making it up. Janet asks me the same thing 'When is it over?' 'When does it end?'

Obviously it never 'ends.' But I've been thinking about that this year.

I do feel like the raw, numb-but-zinging pain mellows a bit around two years. I think that might be true. It's like the infamous year-of-firsts we all hear about passes (and thank God for that), then you stand looking at your year two mountain.

By the time year three comes around, you have a better handle on it - you've begun to establish new traditions, you've come up with people or activities to help fill some of the silence, you don't feel so displaced from your own life.

I was always so surprised at how stupid Jer's passing made me feel. It just felt like I didn't really belong anywhere and no one knew what to do with me. My very presence made people feel uncomfortable ('Yikes, she's the sad one') and they weren't sure what to do or say or how sad I might be ('She seems fine today, don't remind her'). They just got that look on their face and I hated that.

That doesn't happen so much anymore. I think as others settle into the new me - the me without Jer, without a husband - they start acting more normal which helps me feel more normal. That helps us all.

You know how you have those moments when someone

mentions a date that is significant to you, you can't help but make a mental note of it? 'Hey that's my birthday' 'That's my anniversary,' 'That's my mom's birthday.'

Your brain can't help it. You don't say anything as your audience doesn't really care but you notice it. People casually schedule meetings, set up orthodontist appointments or suggest an interview date without knowing that date is significant to you.

The first two years after Jer died, March 1 landed on the weekend - a Friday (I took the day off) and Sunday. This year, March 1 landed on a Monday - the first Monday of the month - a perfectly respectable time to be scheduling meetings, interviews and appointments.

March 1 was stamped on products as an expiration date, it was a suggested date for my job interview, it was filled with meetings at my current job, piano lessons for Victoria etc.

These important dates can still take the wind of out my sails - for days - though now it's less overt. It's subtle, often manifested as fatigue, general blahness, irritability. As you read those symptoms, you know that a lot of things hide in that disguise so it's tricky to spot. But if I'm feeling off, I've learned to just pay attention to the dates and see where I am in my journey through another year.

"I've been surprised how much this week / few weeks / anniversary has taken it out of me. I'm just exhausted - low-grade, constant exhaustion. It's like a hangover - an emotional hangover."

I did take the day off work this year, because I was able to. I scheduled my massage, I scheduled time to write and I always go to the cemetery.

I've done a version of that pretty much every March 1. But I quickly learned that I can't remove myself from life every time there is a significant date with Jer's life and death - days like his birthday, his death date, our anniversary.

The most challenging part for me is those are the days I have to share him. I have to share Jeramy on his birthday and his death day and I'll be honest, I don't like it. Those are the days that others might express how much they miss him. Those are the days others may post photos and/or make a public comment. It makes for a long week(s) as there's no telling when during the week, that someone will post.

I can be clipping along just fine, take a minute to thumb through Instagram and BAM, there's my sweetheart's face - out of the blue - looking back at me. It zings me every time, even still. Right there in the middle of all the mundane, there's my photogenic sweetheart who almost leaps out of every photo, staring back at me while someone writes about how amazing he was and how much they miss him.

I know that the concept of 'sharing' isn't rational from a mathematics standpoint but my heart has never been much for numbers anyway.

I've had to talk myself off the ledge, in a manner of speaking, when these tributes start rolling in. I have to tell myself 'he was a lot of things to a lot of people, they miss him too, it's okay.' It's just hard. It makes for a very long week, walking around in anticipation of an electric shock that you know is coming, you just don't know when.

Actually to pause on this point for one more minute I'm thinking about this concept of managing grief and loss in this digital existence, in the day and age of social media. Others can publicly share what they're feeling that day - sadness at missing your person - and they can do so without any warning, certainly without your permission. It's easier for me when it's someone I also know well - Jer's sister, for instance. It's much harder when it's someone close to Jer but foreign to me, like his friends I've only met once or twice before.

Strange we can exist in a world where people don't bring up the loss of your person to your face, they'd never do that. They don't call when they're thinking about him to check on me, they just do a big post on social media and move on and I'm left trying to get myself back on track.

Not only that, Google and Facebook are great at reminding you of past moments in your life too. 'We thought you'd like this memory,' 'We made you this video.' How intrusive, right? Would you show up at someone's house unannounced and say 'Look at this scrapbook of when your life was happier.' No, you wouldn't.

So while Jeramy was a lot of things to a lot of people, it's a bit like living in an obstacle course during those weeks - I never know when the next hit will be. Those zingers can happen on a random Wednesday, during a random week too; that's harder, I'm less prepared for those.

At any rate, does grief lift? Does the season of grieving end, giving way to a new hopeful life?

I'm hesitant to say that I think that it does. I'm hesitant because I don't know what the me at five years, or 10 years will say. Time moves differently. But I do think that it does.

I think with the surrender, the brain settles a bit and existing in your own body is not as much of an anxiety-ridden, heavy place to live.

Some people say it doesn't get easier but we get better at it? Stronger maybe? I certainly hope so - it's an awfully heavy weight to pull through life.

MOVING FORWARD

Hollywood legend and cultural gem, Betty White, died a few weeks shy of her 100th birthday. Headlines and tributes poured in as the country mourned the loss of an icon who was ahead of her time in most respects.

Betty had been married three times, claiming her last husband, Allen, was the "love of her life." The headline read, "Betty's last word was 'Allen.'"

Romantic, huh?

Allen died 30 years before Betty. Thirty years!

Betty would go on to tell Anderson Cooper in an interview (2011) "I had the love of my life. If you've had the best, who needs the rest?"

Again, romantic huh?

The country swooned, and rightfully so. It IS romantic. It IS sweet.

But that puts so much pressure on the rest of us! This is zero commentary on Ms. White. This is a conversation on how our country relishes stories where a widow (ugh) or widower spends the rest of their lives alone, not interested in remarrying. Or what about the stories where the widower goes to visit the grave every single day until their last?

They're terrific stories and of course should be celebrated.

But so should the stories of a person daring to try again. A person willing to give it another go. The people who desire companionship and are willing to risk another heartbreak.

I remember one dinner a few months after Jer had died where the lady told me she'd buried two husbands, "both great men." I left dinner awash in an unfathomable realization that it could happen again!? Twice?! It took me days to recover from that - it just hadn't occurred to me before.

As I've been saying all along, it's all so individual, there is no right or wrong way. There is only getting through. I'd just like more attention brought to the fact that it's okay to have companionship again.

Isn't it?...

Right?

Or is it....

I don't know I'm still working through that part.

When I read about Betty White, I found myself thinking it's not okay to have companionship again because Jeramy was also the love of my life. I, too, had the best so why bother with the rest.

Let me back up a bit.

I never felt a tremendous need to go talk to a therapist about the loss of Jer as I felt really clear on what happened: My husband died unexpectedly and I'm deeply sad. I knew why I was sad. I was also lucky in that I didn't have the additional and complex layers of emotion that might come from another type of death. It was a tragic and heartbreaking turn of events. I felt like I'd go to therapy and say 'I'm sad' and they'd say 'well your husband died and that's to be expected." Then we'd repeat that every week until when?

But this next chapter, this concept of creating a new life for myself where a happy one once stood, that... *That* is something for which I might need the help of a professional.

I just don't know how this part goes and I don't know when and if it's okay and if people will still know I love Jer endlessly, if his family will be offended, if my family will compare them, will Victoria or Jer's daughters care?

It's another exhausting field to navigate in an already taxing obstacle course.

People always say what Jer would have wanted. "Jeramy doesn't want you down here miserable," "Jeramy would want you to be happy." And I think on the surface, we all agree on that.

But something happens when you actually try to start doing those things; finding happiness. That's harder for people. They've been busy living their lives, consumed with their own activities and worries, they haven't watched your struggles. So it can be an easy default to misjudge the passage of time, right? The ol' 'boy she moved on quickly.'

Throughout the whole process I've been envious of couples who got to have those conversations - either they'd been together long enough they had the 'If I die before you, I'd want you to remarry,' or they endured an illness together and had time for that 'You need to go on and find happiness,' conversation.

I've talked to some friends who have had the family of their dead spouse say 'you need to move forward and find someone else. You have a lot of love to give and you need to find someone when the time is right - you have our blessing.'

None of those happened for me.

Can you believe I even have one friend who was told by her dead husband's family 'we'd be brokenhearted if you ever remarried.' What cruel shackles to put on someone who is already wrapped in the heaviest weighted blanket.

So, what is the collective, agreed upon opinion on how long a person should wait before dating again?

One year?

Two?

Five?

Never?

It's important we all figure it out as it's like this public manifestation or representation of :

- How true the love was
- How much you loved your person
- How devoted you are are to their memory

But if I could survey our society, I'd ask - what's the appropriate amount of time? What would make you feel good about this person's decision to move on? Kids can drive at 16, vote at 18, drink at 21, adults can date again after ____ months/years?

Perhaps a lot of it is a loss of formality.

For instance, during the Civil War era, there were guidelines: Widows mourned their husbands for two years; mothers mourned their children for one; sisters mourned their brothers for six months. The belief being widows grieved the most.

Not only did they have a set amount of time, they had set attire. Black colors and veils during deep mourning eventually working toward grays and purples. Some even announced their grieving process through various jewelry pieces. It was so clear. Everyone knew what was expected and everyone knew what to expect. Simple.

There were also expected behaviors with widows not participating in life - at all - during deep mourning.

Remember in "Gone With the Wind?" Scarlett, during her mourning period, was at a fundraising dance. Good ol' Rhett Butler asked her to dance, in spite of her traditional black garb, and she leapt at the chance.

Did she draws looks? You bet she did.

Should she have? That's the question. I mean, we're not sitting here judging another time and place in history naturally, but what's the harm in Scarlett twirling around the floor with Rhett?

What are we afraid of? Afraid of someone being happy? Afraid that someone isn't sad? Afraid that they're not as sad as we think they should be? Or that dance means Scarlett never cared about her husband in the first place (hmm... Scarlett may not be the best example here).

I'm never comparing grief - ever. The losses are too personal, and too important to even try. But losing a spouse has a unique added nuance - and yes, some could call it an opportunity - of navigating a future with a possible 'replacement.'

As a child in our grief group once noted "you can find another husband, I can't find another dad."

True.

Also, not true.

Suppose for a moment, in a few years' time, that child's mom did find someone new. Suppose that man loved the kid as his own son who, in turn, learned to love that man as a father? That's a beautiful thing, no? That child will not endure any of the judgment that his mom likely did when being gifted with a companion.

It's daunting. It's also utterly public. Sure one can keep things off social media. But it's public in the way that you still have to move through your life - your family will know, your neighbors and, if you're lucky, your friends and eventually coworkers will. Authentically, you can't open your heart to pursue a new chapter and keep it a secret at the same time.

Early on, if asked about dating again or finding someone else I couldn't tell if I was going to puke or punch something. I couldn't tell - just bile in my throat at the mere suggestion. Gross.

My new-agey friend went to a psychic for her own guidance and said Jer showed up. The psychic brought up "you've lost a friend." The psychic confirmed Jer's age and that he had two daughters. According to my friend, the psychic insisted, I am "not to be alone. She is not to be alone." She said Jer was emphatic about that. This was still at a time when I thought I would punch or puke so I teared up and went on about my business.

But I've not forgotten it.

Am I not to be alone? I've never thought I handled it very well. I mean I can do it and I'm fine but long stretches are not good for me - it makes me low.

Jeramy's death has given me a great appreciation for my for my time with people - the merriment and fun; my extraordinary friends. It's also made me appreciate my quiet time, my time alone with my thoughts, my music, my musings. I need it.

But when you're heading out to see a movie alone, or racking your brain to figure out who would go to this concert with you, or wanting desperately to get away for the weekend but everyone in your life has obligations and lives and they can't do impromptu road trips. That's when the yearning for a companion creeps in.

Everyone I know has offered to fill that vacant spot for me on various outings. But that's not the point. Nor is it the same. It's wanting a person, someone who is up for adventures with you, someone who will say yes, someone who is not neglecting their own life to do so and/or is not just trying to make sure you're not sad.

Companionship. It's nice, I like it. How on earth did Betty White go for 30 years without a best friend/lover/true companion?!

DANIEL

Daniel called me after hearing about Jeramy's passing. I knew him through work, as an acquaintance at conferences for years. I didn't want to talk to him. I didn't want to hear the old "I'm sorry for your loss," nonsense. Just not interested. But it was nice of him to reach out (so few do at this time) so I took his call.

Yes he was sorry for my loss, but he also shared that he lost his dad when he was just 16 years old. We had a brief but nice conversation about loss, unexpected loss and I appreciated he had some experience with the havoc it wreaks in one's life.

Daniel would text from time to time to see how I was doing. He lived in a different state so it was never much more than a text or two, but I appreciated the thought.

Time marched on and I continued making my way through my tunnel.

During that time and unbeknownst to me, Daniel's life was experiencing its own upheaval as he and his wife were divorcing and trying to figure out what that looked like for them and their daughters.

By the time that was moving forward, Daniel was texting me more often. *Huh...* In my long, lonely nights and weekends, *doo-*

doo-doo, there came the chirp on my phone, and there came a smile to my face.

Simple at first, little hellos, funny quips and such. Then we texted about divorce, sometimes death, we texted about the odd news happening in our two states, we texted about shows we had seen, landlords and 'next time we're together we need to go here,' or 'you'd love such and such, we should go sometime.' *Huh...*

Then we tried a FaceTime conversation. I made sure I had good lighting and that my hair looked tousled. I couldn't tell if I was trying to look pretty or just not ragged, but I noted it. *Why would I want to look pretty if I'm clearly still in love with Jer and might punch something. So... that doesn't make sense...* Also, dating sounded gross.

But I liked the company. I liked the chirp on my phone. Yes I was still sad to my core, I was still journaling, still visiting the grave, still having moments where tears broke through the surface, but when my phone chirped, I liked it. It was just... nice.

I thought that could be enough. I could mourn the loss of my husband, and just have this friend I text. I felt comfortable with that. *I'll just do that for the next 50 years.*

The weekend that Daniel's wife's belongings were to be moved out of the house was approaching and, naturally, he was dreading it - dreading the shift and the emptiness but certainly dreading standing there watching it happen. He didn't want to be there for it. 'Why don't I come visit you?'

Ummm..... What? Come here? To Utah?..... to .... Visit?..... Umm....... Why? Visit me?... No I can't do that...

He brought it up several more times and I'd hem and haw and say something like 'yea we ought to think about that.' Well there's only so long you can think about things until plans need to be made and tickets booked.

"What if we went somewhere?" he asked. Through our

conversations I knew he hadn't seen any of what Southern Utah has to offer. I love it down there - it's one of those places you go and after you catch your breath from the beauty you think to yourself 'why don't I come down here more often?'

Hmm... no I can't do that...

But then I started thinking... *Why not? Why can't I do that? What am I afraid of? What makes me think I can't do that. I love Southern Utah, I hadn't been in ages, and he'd never seen it. I like road trips, maybe it could be fun. Could it? Yikes what if we got in the car together and I felt trapped? Am I going to let him drive the car Jer bought me?*

I decided I ought to run this by my sister. I wanted to know what she thought of a hare-brained scheme of me taking off to Moab with a man she's never heard of and how I could navigate that without mom asking too many questions.

Looking back, I know that running it by my sister was the safest route to present this question to the world: What if there were ever another a man in my life whose company I enjoyed? Running it by my sister would allow me to say 'yea I mean I'm not going obviously,' or 'Yea I mean, I could never do that.' Because frankly, I didn't know the answer to that question myself. I did not know how I was feeling about it. But... a road trip to Moab sounded fun. Right?

I sent my sister a Vox the next day with some type of preamble 'so I need to know what you think cause I might possibly need your help with mom.' As a side note, my mom is not intrusive in the way this reads. She asks questions as an interested mom but when you're a grown daughter who doesn't really know the answers to some of the questions, it makes you not want to answer any at all.

Voxer is the perfect method for leaving such a message as it lets me get my whole thought recorded and out there, gives her whatever time she needs before she responds. You can't get cut off. So I rattled off my scenario - this guy... known for years...

been chatting… weekend in Moab… and I just don't know… And I waited.

Chirp chirp chirp - there was Voxer, there was my sis. She was all for it. She seemed delighted there was a friend (who we referred to as 'Moab' for months) she seemed delighted at the prospect and happy to help me navigate around mom's questions.

I was surprised by the relief I felt. It wasn't the 'permission,' it was enthusiasm. It was actual happiness for me and this new development. Even after I kept trying to explain and justify "I mean it's not some torrid love affair, we'd have separate rooms which makes me feel better cause I'll likely need the down time." She responded, "Even if it is, hell I hope it IS a torrid love affair! It sounds great!"

I just felt like I was being given a hall pass to get out of the classroom of grief for one weekend. Yes I would return, there was still much to learn in the classroom, but I have a weekend pass - hell I might even laugh. Will I laugh?

Turns out I did - lots.

One of the principles I've gleaned in the tunnel, you don't know how something is going to feel until you try it. If it didn't feel good, then you're not ready. If it felt fine, then keep going. Keep doing what feels at least fine, if not better.

I picked Daniel up at the airport and drove about an hour to Spanish Fork. We stopped for lunch and I decided to try letting him drive. I don't love driving, I always prefer the man drive (they usually prefer that too). But I love that car - it feels like a big warm hug from Jer, like a parting gift of comfort and beauty - is it a weird betrayal to let Daniel drive it?

It wasn't, It was okay. He got behind the wheel and after adjusting all the settings (luckily he thought ahead and made sure he set mine before he fiddled with them), we were off. It was okay. I was okay. We drove and chatted, missing our exit to Moab and having to find a safe turn-around point.

The whole weekend was just nice. It was nice to be taken out to dinner. It was nice to walk into a restaurant and hear the hostess say "Two?" Yes - two. There are two of us. The weather was nice and the countryside beautiful.

Daniel was great - He was fun, and generous and chatty. We laughed, we took pictures - he loved southern Utah. I just noticed I felt at ease, which I appreciated. All of my preconceived angst "but what about….. " "but what if I…." just wasn't there. I felt comfortable.

Then I felt guilty. I dropped Daniel off at the airport, got in the car, drove back to my grief classroom and not only was I still sad, now I felt bad. That guilt part comes and goes, but it does lessen.

Several months passed before Daniel made his way back to Utah. By this point, the world was embroiled in COVID-19 which made everything scary and unsure. Travel certainly wasn't top on anyone's list of things to do and even if you did travel, what on earth would you do once you got there?

He made his way back that summer. I did the same thing I did last time - I got nervous and unsure. We certainly couldn't go back to Moab, but I didn't want him here; I felt positive that he should not be in my home, in a space I shared with Jeramy. I already made up a rule for myself that no one would come into my home until I had moved and lived in my own space.

I planned some type of outing - to Park City for a couple of nights, but what about the third? Daniel wanted to cook for me. *Gosh that sounds nice…. I think I'd really like that.* It had been ages (it had been ages in grief years which is worse than dog years).

These moments were good for me. They forced me to gut-check with myself and all my made up rules, to question if they're really serving me and my healing. Daniel was never pushy but he'd bring it up gently from time to time in our planning and I began to give it some serious thought.

Why? Why did I think I had to move first. And, during COVID, with so much uncertainty, who's to say I'll ever move. What if I'm here for several more years? Then what? But what about all my photos of Jer? What about the love notes still stuck to the fridge? What about.......? The list went on and on.

That 4th of July was a particularly strange one. Our society was at its breaking point with COVID fears and restrictions. The country was reeling from the killing of George Floyd, cities went up in smoke during Black Lives Matter demonstrations, and I sat in my driveway alone listening to the fireworks begin. Even Victoria was at her dad's.

I'd never heard fireworks like I did that 4th - I thought the whole Salt Lake Valley was going to go up in smoke. It was full of such life and, was it celebration? Was it a cry for normalcy? I got up and walked to the corner to watch with my neighbors. Just my nice neighbors next door (who I used to hate because they didn't know Jer), the cute family on the corner, the Russians across the street, and me. I desperately wanted someone to share it with. I wanted someone to be sipping with, to chat to the neighbors with, to enjoy this bizarre evening. I wanted a companion. I wanted to feel safe, I wanted to experience life with a partner and yes, maybe have a little bit of fun along the way.

I decided the next day that I needed to address all my false timelines and made-up rules, and invite Daniel over to cook for me. So we had a date. Of course I tidied up, pausing by the photos of Jer. I didn't want them to make Daniel feel bad. But I felt bad taking them down, especially because of another man. That didn't seem right. So I left them. I had already spent the past year making sure there were photos of a person I loved, but not a mausoleum or shrine. I got worried earlier that year when Matty stopped by that he would wonder...'whoa, what's going on in here?' So I have a few pics on the piano, I have a handsome one of Jer over by my glowing salt rock thing and one by the TV. There is a photo strip of us on the fridge, along with two of his love note post-its. I left them.

When Daniel got there, he walked around and looked at each one, smiling. He just looked, he looked at the pics of Victoria too, he just kind of took it all in but said nothing.

"Is it weird?" I finally asked.

"Is what weird?"

"Do the pictures make you feel weird?"

"Not at all," he said. "I like it. They're all happy times," and he gave me a hug.

We went to my grocery store which I enjoyed sharing with him, oddly enough. He pushed the shopping cart, we studied the artisan olive oils, he yukked it up with the butcher. He did bacon-wrapped dates, to start with, a recipe he had found to match an appetizer we fell in love with in Moab.

"What can I do to help?" I asked.

"Your only job is to sit there and look cute, keep our wine glasses full and be in charge of the music," and that's exactly what I did.

We sipped wine, I sat at the bar thumbing through music in my phone, we sang along to some, some were new to him, he would reach over and give me tastes of various bits and pieces.

I had forgotten what it was like to have a man around and I liked it. They bring a different type of energy and presence and I realized, in that moment, that I missed it, terribly - even beyond what I knew.

Of course Jer was also present but not in the way I feared. I thought of him but not in comparison, not at all. Just like you likely don't sit there thinking about turkey while eating an orange. They're different.

I'm making a point of these realizations as it's one of the litmus tests to 'how am I doing?' and it's also something I get asked about most by my friends and certainly fellow grievers: Isn't it weird? Don't you think of Jer the whole time? It can't be the same? It's not; I do but not the whole time; and it's not.

It's not going to be the same because I am not the same. The me today is not the same me who galloped through life next to Jer. That was a different, lighter, less experienced me. The me today has different needs, meaning perhaps someone else could step in and fill those? In a relationship, we grow and morph - hopefully together. Without Jer, I've still grown and morphed so perhaps another *could* fill that role?

I guess I would also argue, the goal is not to create the same thing and I'm intrigued by that notion when it comes to spouses or partners - this one-true-love idea. We don't do that with any other relationships in our lives. We don't think we have one-true-kid and therefore never have another. When we have the second or third, we do not worry that the world will think we didn't love the first one all that much. We also don't worry and wonder how you'll ever create another kid who is exactly like the first, because that's not the goal. Creating and raising individuals is the goal.

Can we shift our mindset that it's okay for people to create and raise individual relationships and one is not a reflection of how much someone loved the other?

I was widowed. I lost the love of my life at a tragically early age, when our dream life together was just beginning. I will love Jeramy always. There will always be a piece of my heart that belongs to him and no one else. I will always say prayers of gratitude for my time with him, that I was loved like that, that I experienced a few moments spinning in his presence. It's a gift beyond measure.

I am a package deal - Me and this chunk of my heart that is Jeramy's. There was a scene in Season 2, Episode 1 of the Amazon Prime show, "Modern Love." Again, sorry for spoilers, but the wife is in her second marriage, having lost her first husband.

She asked her current husband if it ever bothered him or did he know how much she thought of her first husband. Not only did it not bother him, he said "Your heart was the biggest place I'd ever been in the world." He knew even a little bit of her heart would be an extraordinary amount of love. I wept. I had to pause the show because I couldn't see it through my tears. What a beautiful statement. And I needed that line at that moment.

Just like we share our hearts with our second and third child, just like we can love multiple nieces and nephews, just like we can love a new dog, perhaps differently but just as fiercely, and just like loving more than one friend, our hearts can grow. They can grow enough to encompass all the people we care for.

There is something truly extraordinary, almost sacred, about the person who can look at the package deal and accept all of the deal. The person who is willing to hold space - allowing room for that sweet spot in your heart to exist in this world. The person who is not bothered by photos, the person who knows you'll want to celebrate special days and moments but might need quiet on other days. The person who believes in your heart's capacity to grow and change shape, to love them along with your other person. That is special.

SIX YEARS

Daniel and I continued for a time; FaceTiming, laughing, and planning trips. He listened while I played guitar, and he liked knowing when I was home safe. It was nice. I liked having someone vested in my life and its twists and turns.

Eventually, which you probably gathered from the past tense, he and I went our separate ways, the distance proving too great. But what a profoundly important chapter for me - a chapter to prove that I would and could feel things again. People told me that I would, but I was surprised to actually feel it for myself.

In 2024, we passed the six-year mark of Jeramy's passing. Now he's been gone twice as long as I knew him.

Weird, isn't it?

I always knew he'd eventually end up being a small blip on my life's radar. If the Medium is right, and I'm down here a long time (which I hope I am) three years is a small blip of time.

Over the past three years, I got a new job which allows me to better support my daughter (thankful for that). I was sent through a different tunnel and came out the other side of a breast cancer diagnosis and treatment (supremely thankful for that) and I had the most amazing 'I'm Still Standing' celebration party! I posted that I'd be hanging out at a certain neighborhood bar for the evening and I'll be danged if people from all the chapters of my life didn't show up with big smiles and hugs.

I bought a home with private backyard space yet still often sit in the driveway - what can I say? I've gotten used to watching the world go by. I visited Peru and Paris, we hauled all the cousins to Disneyland (twice), Matty and I made it back to New York (we saw four shows), I got to visit Vietnam for an amazing work opportunity and I ventured off to the Mediterranean, finally seeing Greece and Italy, two dream destinations of mine.

I still go to the cemetery. I still write. I still work on songwriting and finally dared to start sharing my original songs on my social channels (@ericahansen13 on Instagram) and would love to perform them live someday.

I sit here absolutely delighted that I'm not just thinking about a future, but am hopeful for it too. For the longest time I could not say that.

You, reading this book, are part of that hope. Jeramy always wanted us to write our story. And I did it. This is our story and now you're a part of it too. We love you for that.

Afterword

Write. Journal. I mean it.

When I learn of someone's passing, well first, I gasp, then my go-to token gift is a card and a journal. I write something like "journaling helped me process. It helped me put words to feelings etc etc"

It helps. It doesn't just help me but has been proven to help, well, everyone.

There is something about the process of writing the words "I'm sad," "This feels unfair," "Why me?" "How could you?" "Where are you?" "Did you see what happened today?" "I miss you."

In my circle, very few believe it will be helpful and very few have taken my advice. They say "yea but you're a writer. I don't process things that way." While that may be true, in part, it's not about writing. It's about spending time with yourself. It's about allowing yourself the time to think about what you're feeling. It's about putting words to those feelings.

My sister and I, both moms of teenage daughters, have had to work with our teens on identifying or being able to pinpoint what they're feeling. "What are you feeling? Sadness? Frustration? Disappointment? Anger?"

Even as adults, it's difficult to do. We avoid the unpleasant, we distract ourselves. We tend to not want to sit with ourselves, especially if it's in sadness. As though sitting and admitting we're sad will actually make us sadder.

There are countless books on grief, sadness, and journaling written by people with more degrees than I have. But I can tell you writing allows your brain to stop and acknowledge it's been enduring something difficult and yet is still keeping you alive. It allows your cells to take a breath. It gives your heart a moment to focus on itself as well. It's a form of self-care that includes your entire self - it gives all of you a chance to pause and say 'hey... this really hard thing happened and we're all still here. We are enduring, we (we meaning all your organs and cells) we need a moment to breathe, to check in, to feel and to release.'

It's hard to do those things in our rapid-fire lifestyle. It's hard to do those things when the grief is crushing and you hate everything about everything. But that's exactly when you open your journal, click your favorite pen and write "I hate everything about everything!!!" Draw angry faces, fill it with swear words if that's where your heart takes you.

I guess it's a little bit like letting yourself have a good cry. We avoid it, we don't want to, crying makes us sad, and yet once you cry and let some of that sorrow out of your system, we tend to sit up, take a deep breath and feel better.

One of my grieving girlfriends said "I don't want to journal it's so sad." And it is. But the sadness is there no matter what you're doing, kind of hanging over your head like all those projects you keep meaning to get to. You've got to take the time to actually *feel* the sadness, to allow you brain the chance to set down some of what it's carrying for you, and that's difficult. But journaling gets some of that sorrow on paper and out of you.

My theory (which I've since researched the science to back it up) the grief stays in your body, buried in your cells, until you consciously work on releasing it. If you ignore it or avoid it, the sadness just stays in there and turns brown. Rots? It just turns brown and stagnant and remains as an extra weight you always have to carry around making you and everything about you, sluggish.

In one of the relationship books I read many moons ago, they talked about giving men a chance to 'go back to the well.' Meaning, you ask them something or say something and they'll give you their first and quickest response. If you pause, rather than charging ahead with your next thought, it allows them time to 'go back to the well,' they will find more information.

Which brings me back to that quote I love - *"I write because I don't know what I think until I read what I say."* Journaling about

Jeramy's death has not only helped me process, it's helped me get to know myself on a whole new level. Journaling is my way of letting myself go back to the well to find more information. There is always uncertainty as I start turning that crank to see what comes up in the bucket, but the anticipation is scarier than what's actually in there and as soon as I have it, I can name it, remove it from the bucket and see what else I have inside.

If you're standing at the beginning of the tunnel, are somewhere in the middle, actually if you just want to make more sense of life, take your journal with you - you'll be surprised to read how far you've progressed.

Acknowledgements

When I talk about the people holding the puzzle pieces to put me back together again, many of those same people were doing the same with this book.

Laura - One of my closest souls; a supreme believer in possibility who understands living for the hope of it all and someone who endured countless, countless, conversations, drafts and what-ifs and what-abouts as this book came to life. I simply could not have done it without you.

Jamie - Another of my closest souls and a top-notch proofreader, thought-provoker and steady support. Thank you for your interest and encouragement.

Mom and Dad - What can I say? Thank you for the early read-through. Thank you for your support. Thank you for loving Jer the way you did. Thank you for all the meals.

Matty - You're the best. My gratitude for you, and our friendship, knows no bounds. Let's go get a burrito and celebrate.

Jodi and Jill - Your place in this story and my life were and are exceptionally important. Thank you.

Dawn - Thank you. Again, and always, thank you.

Lisa - Your wonderful encouragement and guidance helped me believe I am actually a writer. Thank you for sharing your wisdom with me.

To my astounding friends who not only buoy me up in life, but are always asking "what's going on with your book?" I love you all - Jessica, Christina, Michele, Marcia, Kirsten, Hannah, Julie, Kennedy, Bruce, Scott and Scot.

To the Evans family - I love you. Thank you for sharing Jer with me.

To my fam - I love you all beyond measure. Thank you for being a wonderful support system, encouraging me to keep putting myself out there, and for eating my baked goods on Sundays.

ABOUT THE AUTHOR

Erica Hansen

Erica Hansen has always been writing something - from newspaper articles, to blog posts, to press releases. How lovely to finally add 'book' to that list. She's a communications professional by day, and a musician, songwriter and dreamer by night. She lives in Salt Lake City with her fantastic daughter.
Instagram: @ericahansen13
To hear music refererenced in the book, visit www.theericahansen.com

www.ingramcontent.com/pod-product-compliance
Lightning Source LLC
Chambersburg PA
CBHW021220130626
46554CB00004B/1298